THE WESLEYAN THEOLOGY SERIES

Holiness

Diane Leclerc
Floyd Cunningham

D1707633

THE FOUNDRY
PUBLISHING

The Foundry Publishing®
PO Box 419527
Kansas City, MO 64141
thefoundrypublishing.com

978-0-8341-4311-1

Printed in the
United States of America

Cover Design: Arthur Cherry
Interior design: Sharon Page

Library of Congress Cataloging-in-Publication Data
A complete catalog record for this book is available from the Library of Congress.

The internet addresses, email addresses, and phone numbers in this
book are accurate at the time of publication. They are provided as a
resource. The Foundry Publishing does not endorse them or vouch for
their content or permanence.

10 9 8 7 6 5 4 3 2 1

For Janice Elder
The other Cunningham sibling
Also a published author, and our unwavering supporter

Contents

Introduction
Another Book on Holiness?

It was revealed to [the prophets] that they were not serving themselves but you, when they spoke of the things that have now been told you by those who have preached the gospel to you by the Holy Spirit sent from heaven. Even angels long to look into these things.

Therefore, with minds that are alert and fully sober, set your hope on the grace to be brought to you when Jesus Christ is revealed at his coming. As obedient children, do not conform to the evil desires you had when you lived in ignorance. But just as he who called you is holy, so be holy in all you do; for it is written: "Be holy, because I am holy."

—1 Peter 1:12–16

A reader opening the pages of this book who is unfamiliar with the ideas of holiness and sanctification will hopefully find this material to be accessible and graspable. On the other hand, readers who are already very familiar with these concepts might rightly wonder, *Why yet another book on holiness?* The most direct reason is that the publisher has created a much-needed series of books on theological topics from a Wesleyan-Holiness perspective. A professional theologian will immediately notice that the titles in this series line up under the usual topics covered in any systematic theology. One way to study our understandings about God, humanity, and salvation is to approach them topically in this manner. A typical systematic theology begins with explaining how we *do* theology and then moves, broadly speaking, to the doctrines concerning God, Christ, the Spirit, and the church. Under these, there are subtopics that are also keenly important, such as the Trinity, the atonement, the doctrine of sin, the sacraments, and beliefs about Christ's return, to name a few.

Every good systematic theology puts God at the center, unifying the system. Different theological traditions emphasize different subcategories specifically as essential to the ethos of that tradition. The doctrine of salvation—the question of how we can be saved and live as Christians— has a central position in the Wesleyan-Holiness tradition, and a subcategory under salvation has been considered essential to our identity: the theology of holiness and sanctification. It would be inconceivable to produce a series of systematic theology books in the Wesleyan tradition and not have a book on holiness. For the denominations born out of the Holiness Movement, this doctrine is the unifying, distinctive spiritual reality that sustains our identity; indeed, it is our "watchword and song."[1]

There are secondary reasons why another book on holiness can be helpful in our present time. First, there is still great confusion about holiness theology—in our classrooms, in our pulpits, and especially in our pews. We are not the same movement that began more than a hundred years ago. Although there is so much to treasure about the early days—the revivals and camp meetings, where the urgency of entire sanctification was preached; the unity and cooperation of denominational development seen in affiliations and mergers; the grassroots nature of our churches that extended into our local and global emphasis on missions—the context we live in today is light-years away from those pioneering days of national and industrial expansion

---

1. This phrase comes from the hymn "Holiness unto the Lord," written by Lelia N. Morris in 1900. It appears in the Nazarene hymnal *Sing to the Lord* and is considered the unofficial theme song for the Church of the Nazarene. *Our Watchword and Song* is also the title of the centennial history of the denomination, written by Stan Ingersol, Floyd T. Cunningham, and Harold E. Raser.

and development. It could be argued that we need to recapture the fervor and vision of our forefathers and mothers. But we need new wineskins to hold a revival of passion and compassion.

Part of what is needed in holiness theology and practice today is a translation of the truth into new language and metaphors that are fitting and effective for our contemporary situation. Let us imagine a theological spectrum. On one side, we find the belief that God reveals truth to us in a particular and unchanging form and language. The cultural and historical context, then, matters very little. On the opposite side of the spectrum is the position that context *determines* truth—to the point that truth could change depending on the situation. Is there a good *via media*—a good Wesleyan term that means a "middle way"—between these poles? There is. This more central idea believes in the universal truth of holiness and the spiritual reality of sanctification. We believe that the call to holiness is true for everyone at every time. The context does not change the spiritual reality of the gift of sanctifying grace God gives to us. This is an essential for Wesleyans. *How* that essential is communicated is key. Antiquated language and metaphors will fall on deaf ears. Holiness lives and breathes in whatever context in which it finds itself, for it transcends contextual underpinning. Yet this transcendent and vital message must be translated into whatever cultural or generational context we are addressing. The correlational task between truth and context is never complete. The truth of holiness remains constant, but this truth must be articulated to differing contexts so that it is communicated effectively.

This correlation is not only crucial in light of the passing from one historical era to the next but also from one global culture to another. Sensitivity has been raised of late to the theological colonialism that transpired through earlier decades in our history. In some cases, an Americanized articulation was forced on very non-American cultures. Now we understand the repercussions of such a thoughtless strategy. We now see openness to the truth of the holiness message when appropriately expressed through individualized and contextualized cultural vernacular, metaphors, and idioms.

An aspect of our time is the recognition of globalization. The churches of the Holiness Movement have begun appropriately to envision themselves in the context of the global church, which necessarily includes theological cross-pollination. A one-way delivery system is not acceptable. Does this mean we are changing the spiritual reality of God's sanctifying grace? Absolutely not. We are broadening our understanding of how it can penetrate every culture by allowing it to do so! The same can be said about generational cultures. New language meets younger ears; they need to be freed to put the truth of holiness into language that captures and resonates with persons who were not even alive in the twentieth century, let alone the nineteenth.

There is a second concern and reason for this book's exploration of holiness. I had the privilege of serving as a representative of my denomination for three years on a consultation committee known as the Wesleyan Holiness Study Project. The committee was commissioned to strategize ways to promote the message of holiness in the twenty-first century—no small task. As this committee—made up of theologians and ecclesiastical leaders from a number of Holiness denominations—gathered, it quickly became clear that we shared a common anxiety about the future of holiness. Some labeled this concern a crisis. Rather than a crisis over the different ways to express entire sanctification, it was seen as a crisis of silence. The danger we saw in those meetings was the risk of lacking *any* articulation. The concern is not about holiness being preached this way or

that way but about whether it is being preached or understood *at all.*

Pastors and leaders of our current era have been
compelled by the pressing demands of changing culture
to focus on the latest *method* at the expense of the holiness
message. We recognize that churches in North America are
losing ground as membership drops, not only in mainline
churches but in Holiness denominations as well. "In the
process of trying to lead growing, vibrant churches, our
people have become largely ineffective and fallen prey to a
generic Christianity that results in congregations that are
indistinguishable from the culture around them. Churches
need a clear, compelling message" of holiness for today.[2]
For the young and the old, there is a need to clear up confusion and make, as John Wesley himself put it, a "plain
account of Christian perfection." Yet it is absolutely crucial
that the next generations hear the message of holiness clearly. They need to experience holiness, live it, understand it,
and be able to communicate and teach it into the future.
Only as new generations grasp it with heart and mind will
the message of holiness continue to make a true difference
in the world to come. Holiness is always relevant!

A third reason for this book comes in the wake of the
new issues the church faces today that have no precedent
in the recent past. The Holiness Movement's continued
relevance and potential influence on these issues is pressing. The fear that this book will be rendered obsolete by
focusing on societal concerns is tempered by an almost
universal agreement that they will be seen by future historians as having lasting significance. Interestingly, there
are many similarities between matters and disputes today
and those faced at the beginning of the Wesleyan-Holiness

2. Kevin W. Mannoia and Don Thorsen, eds., *The Holiness Manifesto* (Grand
Rapids: Eerdmans, 2008), 19.

Movement. And so, even as we strongly affirm the need for new translations of holiness to fit our present context, we also know we are not plowing completely new ground. The question is whether we are willing to learn from our past. Regrettably, so many members of Holiness denominations are disconnected from and unaware of their faith heritage and history.

The chapters that follow address many different aspects of Wesleyan-Holiness theology. We will begin by exploring the difference between holiness and sanctification. We will also explore themes that have been crucial to our identity in the past and that continue to be relevant today. How does the metaphor of cleansing relate to the holy life? What is morality? What is the purpose of holiness in our lives? Where does the Holy Spirit fit into our holiness paradigm? Does sanctification affect our character over time? What does it mean to love God and others? How does holiness relate to pain and suffering? Finally, how might we unleash our theology to meet the problems and concerns of the present world?

The Holiness Movement has, historically and theologically, had keen insight into the spiritual reality of a life entirely devoted to God. Our focus on surrender, consecration, and sacrificial living are key activities, aided by the Spirit. Even more specifically, we have traditionally associated these synonyms for surrender with the experience of entire sanctification. Entire sanctification has a theological context that this book hopes to illuminate. We would be in error if we did not recognize that this type of obedient surrender is hard. Yet we must also recognize that it is not a harsh message; it is not an austere life of drudgery to which we are called. The life of holiness is anything but severe, stark, or bleak. The holiness message is one of vitality, energy, strength, depth, joy, transformation, spiritual power, and *agape* love. Jesus's words do not *only* call us to lose our lives; he also promises that we will truly find life in him. In Hebrew, the term *l'chaim* is a salute "to life!" May holiness and sanctification not just be doctrines in a book but truly a call *to life* in its fullness.

One last note. I am pleased to have my brother, Floyd Cunningham, PhD, join me here in writing a couple of chapters and parts of chapters of this book. He is the expert in the history of the Church of the Nazarene. He is a church historian by training and has insight into the Holiness Movement and the sum of all of the history of the church since the apostles. He spent his entire career teaching in an Asian context. He just retired from his position at Asia-Pacific Nazarene Theological Seminary after forty years. I guess our parents, who never had the opportunity to go to college, did something right. I am a historical theologian, and Floyd is a church historian. We are both ordained elders, both previous pastors of churches, and both deeply devoted to the best of our tradition as professors and preachers. We have served in ministry for a combined total of seventy-five years. This is our first attempt to write something together. It is fitting that it is a book on holiness, which is indeed our watchword and song.

A Journey through the Sermon on the Mount

The Paradox of Holy Living

ONE

We begin with a scriptural study of holiness by examining the Sermon on the Mount at some length. Although the words "holiness" and "sanctification" do not appear in the sermon, Jesus's teachings in Matthew 5–7 certainly depict a holy life. We find here the most concise expression of Jesus's holy ethics. We find not only sins to avoid but also holy actions of love that we are expected to express. Jesus even delves into our very core motivations and attitudes. The Beatitudes explore what it means to have a holy heart, out of which all our deeds flow. The Sermon on the Mount, and holiness theology in general, show us the paradoxical nature of Christian living. Despite our present circumstances, which can be grim, even dire, there can still be transformation and victory through the grace of God.

Holiness as Perfection

In order to understand Matthew 5, which begins the famous Sermon on the Mount, it would do us well to look at the end of the chapter before we look at the beginning, for it gives us the overarching theme for the entire sermon. Matthew 5:48 reads: "Be perfect, therefore, as your heavenly Father is perfect." The Sermon on the Mount is a call to sanctification and holiness, sometimes called "Christian perfection." Matthew 5:48 is a significant verse in the Wesleyan tradition, yet perfection is certainly one of the most misunderstood theological words in the history of the Wesleyan-Holiness Movement!

Why not abandon the word altogether? Does it function in any positive way today? Is it worth maintaining in light of all the misconceptions that surround it? Wesley himself faced steady opposition to the doctrine in his own day, which led him to consider whether he should drop it, or make a point of it. He decided to make a point of it because it is a *biblical* word. "Be perfect as your heavenly Father is perfect" cannot be easily brushed aside. (We will deal with perfection at length in chapter 8.)

There are two primary ways to understand this command of Jesus. First, we could see Jesus as a great motivational speaker. He sets before the disciples the apparently impossible goal of perfection as a way of motivating them. Like a carrot tied to a pole just out of a donkey's reach, we are motivated to at least keep moving in the right direction even if we never get there. *Or*, we can believe Jesus actually meant what he said—that we really are to be in some way "perfect," and that we really can be more like him in this life. Wesleyans choose this second understanding. When God calls us to holiness, God means it.

A short biblical review of the Greek words translated as "perfection" reveals multiple nuances that are often missed in English. When we think of perfection in the English language, we imagine an absolute sense of flawlessness. But most Greek words that are translated as "perfect" or "perfection" have more nuanced meanings like "maturity," "completeness," "fullness," or "wholeness." At times they imply that we are fulfilling the purpose or end that God intends for us—namely, love. They are used in a few places to contrast mature Christians with immature Christians, or new Christians. In other places they imply that we are found qualified by the grace of God. They rarely indicate good conduct, particularly in a legalistic way; rather, the Greek word most often means the quality of our character—where good conduct comes out of who we are. If there is any passage in the New Testament that speaks of godly character, it is the Sermon on the Mount. It is thoroughly a holiness text that begins with the Beatitudes.

The Beatitudes

The passage where we find the Beatitudes is probably one of the most well-known parts of Scripture. Their form is not unique; examples of it can be found both in Greek and Hebrew literature. What makes the Beatitudes unique is their *paradoxical* nature. Jesus describes a particular situation or quality of a person, announces that such a person is blessed, and speaks of a particular outcome that counters their present circumstances. They seem pretty straightforward, but their interpretation is vigorously debated. One interpretation is that Jesus is shining a light on human sin and the need for grace. The only response in light of this interpretive model would be repentance of our own inadequacy to live by kingdom principles.

Other interpretations question whether Jesus is speaking descriptively or normatively. In other words, is he simply describing the situation in the life to come for those who suffer presently—the attitudes listed are far beyond our reach and speak in terms of otherworldly fulfillment? Or is he suggesting that these are qualities we are to pursue presently that require our obedient attitudes and actions *now*? Is he promising persons who are *literally* poor, mournful, oppressed, and hungry that God sees them and will change their earthly fate in our eternal life? Or is he speaking more spiritually, calling his disciples (which includes us) to change their hearts and lives? The Sermon on the Mount, as interpreted through the lens of Wesleyan-Holiness theology, makes this tradition distinct from other traditions by strongly suggesting that its ethics are to be lived now, as we are changed and empowered by the Holy Spirit. Timothy Smith, one of the most important historians and interpreters of the Wesleyan-Holiness movement, says the belief that the sermon can indeed be lived is a dividing line between it and most other evangelicals.[1]

Certainly we should not simply read the Beatitudes passively today, as if we are not implicated by their wisdom and power. We cannot sit on the sidelines and think Jesus is speaking to another era. Another way to phrase the key question invoked by Christ's radical words is whether we believe that we can be holy in this life, or only in the life to come. Crucial is the recognition that the wisdom of the Beatitudes specifically, and the Sermon on the Mount more generally, is a hard truth. In the words of Pinchas Lapide, "The history of the impact of the Sermon on the Mount can be largely described in terms of an attempt to domesticate everything in it that is shocking, demanding, and uncompromising, and render it harmless" by believing that the words have little relevance for us today.[2] Will we allow its truth to confront us in ways that change us? Jesus turns everything upside down by describing people of the kingdom in utterly unexpected ways.

Who Is Blessed?

Blessed are the poor in spirit, for theirs is the kingdom of heaven.
Blessed are those who mourn, for they will be comforted.
Blessed are the meek, for they will inherit the earth.
Blessed are those who hunger and thirst for righteousness, for they will be filled.
Blessed are the merciful, for they will be shown mercy.

---

1. Floyd T. Cunningham, "Common Ground: The Perspective of Timothy L. Smith on American Religious History," *Fides et Historia* (Summer/Fall 2012): 23.

2. Pinchas Lapide, *The Sermon on the Mount: Utopia or Program for Action?* (Maryknoll, NY: Orbis Books, 1986), 4.

Blessed are the pure in heart, for they will see God.
Blessed are the peacemakers, for they will be called children of
God.

—Matthew 5:3–9

In Luke 4, we find the story of Jesus reading from the scroll in the synagogue of his own hometown. He read from Isaiah 61. When he finished, he proclaimed, "Today this scripture is fulfilled in your hearing" (v. 21). The people were angry and aggressive in the end. What did Jesus say that agitated them to the point of chasing him, hoping to throw him over a cliff (vv. 28–29)?

First, Jesus shook the people's imaginations by announcing that the Year of Jubilee—"the year of the Lord's favor" (v. 19)—is a reality. In the Old Testament, the Year of Jubilee was to come every fifty years. Forty-nine years is seven times seven. Not only were the people to rest every seventh day, but they were also to rest every seven years by, for example, leaving their crops unfurrowed. During these forty-nine-year periods, the people could expand the lands and their fortunes by having others be in debt to them. But in the fiftieth year, everyone was supposed to return land and money to their original owners. Debts would be forgiven. Everything would be reversed. It would be a day filled with restoration. Interestingly, we do not have any biblical or historical proof that Jubilee was ever actually celebrated. Such a reversal would favor the poor and those who had been taken advantage of, so it would not have been popular with the powerful.

Second, Jesus took a messianic passage and implied that he himself was the Messiah. Their hometown boy was blaspheming! Blaspheming meant to call oneself God, or equate oneself with God. It was punishable by death—and, as we know, Jesus was eventually put to death for this crime. The irony here is, of course, that Jesus really *was* God. What Isaiah 61 says that Jesus claimed as his mission was that when the Messiah came, he would bring good news to the poor, freedom for the captive, sight for the blind, release for the oppressed; the Messiah would bring the Jubilee, in other words. And the Messiah would call his followers to minister to these oppressed groups.

Some scholars believe that what Jesus says in Luke 4, quoting Isaiah 61, is found in the Beatitudes as ethical teaching. The kingdom does not belong to whom we might expect. The "least of these" (see Matthew 25:40) will be given the kingdom of heaven, be comforted, and inherit the earth—not the religious elite. The "least of these" will be fulfilled, given grace, granted a vision of God, and be called God's children—not the spiritually arrogant. The Messiah comes to the "least of these"—not to the piously haughty. It is not the rich, the happy, the proud, the gluttonous, the unmerciful, the hypocritical, and the warmongers who are blessed. It is the poor, the mournful, the meek, the hungry, the merciful, the peacemaker, the pure, and the innocent, whom God sees through eyes of love and grace. The poor, imprisoned, blind, and oppressed are driven to complete reliance and absolute dependence on God. They know they cannot save themselves. This is key!

If we want to be part of the kingdom of God, these are the humble attitudes and actions we must pursue. But we should never see them as something we can achieve on our own. It is not as if, when we reach these attitudinal goals, God will respond with blessings. We never *merit* the kingdom. The spirit of the Beatitudes is not some new law, as if by being poor and meek, and so on, we earn the reward of God's favor. It is not a contractual agreement that, if we do our part, God will do God's part. The Beatitudes are predicated on God's grace! Grace precedes any requirements! By grace we are saved, and by grace we are transformed. By grace we are made holy and whole. Grace is the work of the Holy Spirit in our lives to effect ongoing transformation.

If we want to be part of the kingdom of God, these are the humble attitudes and actions we must pursue. But we should never see them as something we can achieve on our own.

Who Really Represents God?

Blessed are those who are persecuted because of righteousness, for theirs is the kingdom of heaven.

Blessed are you when people insult you, persecute you and falsely say all kinds of evil against you because of me. Rejoice and be glad, because great is your reward in heaven, for in the same way they persecuted the prophets who were before you.

You are the salt of the earth. But if the salt loses its saltiness, how can it be made salty again? It is no longer good for anything, except to be thrown out and trampled underfoot.

You are the light of the world. A town built on a hill cannot be hidden. Neither do people light a lamp and put it under a bowl. Instead they put it on its stand, and it gives light to everyone in the house. In the same way, let your light shine before others, that they may see your good deeds and glorify your Father in heaven.

—Matthew 5:10–16

The word "blessed" has sometimes been translated as "happy." "Happy are those who. . ." For English speakers in contemporary Western cultures, happiness often describes a superficial feeling we pursue. It is therefore more appropriate for us to understand the word "blessed" by referring to its Hebrew and Greek meanings, which describe those who find God's favor. It can also mean "human flourishing." Those who are blessed find deep fulfillment in God. It is clear from Scripture that, unlike the modern sense of a happy feeling, blessedness is not based on one's circumstances.

Thus, Paul can write, "I have learned the secret of being content in any and every situation . . . whether living in plenty or in want. I can do all this through him who gives me strength" (Philippians 4:12–13); and James can admonish: "Consider it pure joy, my brothers and sisters, whenever you face trials of many kinds, because you know that the testing of your faith produces perseverance. Let perseverance finish its work so that you may be mature and complete, not lacking anything" (James 1:2–4).

John Wesley connected happiness in its deeper meaning with holiness, believing that the holy life, filled with love and virtue, is the only way to find joy and contentment. It is also imperative to say explicitly that there is no sense of true blessedness for a person outside of relationships and community. This goes for all the implications of holiness. Solitary holiness is an oxymoron—there is no such thing.

An interesting question of interpretation of the Sermon on the Mount is: who is the audience? If we look at the first verses, we assume it is the disciples of Jesus, but the concluding verses imply it is the whole crowd. Yet it does seem that 5:10–16 are directed to the appointed apostles and Jesus's closest followers.

We know from church history that the apostles were persecuted, some to the point of death. John was banished, Stephen was martyred, and Peter was supposedly crucified upside down. Jesus said to the apostles in this Matthew 5 passage that they could expect to be persecuted, just as were the prophets who came before them. Yet he calls them "blessed." What happened to the prophets who came before the apostles? They were killed. By whom? The religious elite who were so convinced of their own perspectives that they could not hear the messages sent by God. Jesus himself was killed by religious men who could not see the very Messiah who stood in front of them. The apostles would suffer the same fate.

Notice that Jesus said they would be persecuted not because they *called* themselves Christ followers but because of their righteousness and their identity with his own character. They were blessed not because they lived comfortable lives under peaceful circumstances but because they followed Jesus in his suffering. This is the paradox of holy living—we can suffer and still live victorious and virtuous lives. We see it in the apostles and in the life of Paul:

> But we have this treasure in jars of clay to show that this all-surpassing power is from God and not from us. We are hard pressed on every side, but not crushed; perplexed, but not in despair; persecuted, but not abandoned; struck down, but not destroyed. We always carry around in our body the death of Jesus, so that the life of Jesus may also be revealed in our body. For we who are alive are always being given over to death for Jesus' sake, so that his life may also be revealed in our mortal body.
> (2 Corinthians 4:7–11)

True holiness is characterized by the humble attitudes and actions described in the Beatitudes and the whole Sermon on the Mount. True holiness is about a spirit of unassuming reliance on God, and about self-giving love. If we are being truly Christian in the world, we will be salt and light. People will be drawn to taste and see that the Lord is good as we reflect the character of Jesus and shine his light in the darkness.

The Standards of Holy Love

The God of holy love desires to make us holy as well. It is absolutely essential, when speaking of human holiness, that we add the word "love." Holiness without love is no holiness at all. If we simply define human holiness as sinlessness, we have defined it only by an absence. There was a time in the Holiness Movement when the absence of sin became the primary goal and emphasis, but holiness is never a passive state, nor does it consist of an empty vacuum. There must be the presence of love in the holy life to which God calls us. Read Ephesians 3:14–19 anew:

> For this reason I kneel before the Father, from whom every family in heaven and on earth derives its name. I pray that out of his glorious riches he may strengthen you with power through his Spirit in your inner being, so that Christ may dwell in your hearts through faith. And I pray that you, being rooted and established in love, may have power, together with all the Lord's holy people, to grasp how wide and long and high and deep is the love of Christ, and to know this love that surpasses knowledge—that you may be filled to the measure of all the fullness of God.

Holiness and love cannot be separated. We can only love others with Christlike love if and when we know ourselves to be loved by a holy God.

Holiness as Relationship

Holiness, abstracted from human relationships, makes no sense. Holiness has everything to do with how we relate to God and others; the very nature of these relationships is founded on love. Disembodied holiness—or holiness as an abstract concept or theological jargon—is always a danger. Disembodiment negates true holiness. Love always cherishes particular relationships and particular humans in real bodies.

It is also dangerous to separate holiness from community. The Christian community is essential to each person's pursuit of holiness and love. There is no such thing as a solitary Christian life. God intends for the church to truly act as one and for each part to be servants to the rest. This is why the majority of Paul's references to love are in the context of the church. Bringing the church together requires genuine love. It is also appropriate to identify the church *as a whole* as holy. The love, then, that is central to a strong Wesleyan-Holiness theology is always interdependent in the context of the body of Christ (see more on this topic in chapter 9.)

While love is essential to the relationships *within* the body of Christ, we are no less responsible for our relationships *outside* the church. As Jesus moves from the Beatitudes to the rest of the Sermon on the Mount, he addresses specific relationships, beginning with the relationship between Mosaic law and holy love.

Surpassing Righteousness

Do not think that I have come to abolish the Law or the Prophets; I have not come to abolish them but to fulfill them. For truly I tell you, until heaven and earth disappear, not the smallest letter, not the least stroke of a pen, will by any means disappear from the Law until everything is accomplished. Therefore anyone who sets aside one of the least of these commands and teaches

others accordingly will be called least in the kingdom of heaven,
but whoever practices and teaches these commands will be called
great in the kingdom of heaven. For I tell you that unless your
righteousness surpasses that of the Pharisees and the teachers of
the law, you will certainly not enter the kingdom of heaven.

—*Matthew 5:17–20*

What Jesus says here, we simply do not expect. We reasonably understand Jesus to be the one to usher in a *new* idea of the kingdom of God, a *new* vision of whom God saves, and a *new* covenant. But Jesus challenges what we expect and speaks of his fidelity to what has come before.

A wrong way to interpret these verses is to misunderstand what Jesus means by "the Law and the Prophets." An incorrect reading infers that we are to obey all 613 laws in the Old Testament, which include dietary restrictions as well as commands that were culturally bound to that time.

Paul's writings make clear that Christians are not required to obey the law in this manner. In Philippians 3:4–9 he writes about himself:

> Though I myself have reasons for such confidence. If someone else thinks they have reasons to put confidence in the flesh, I have more: circumcised on the eighth day, of the people of Israel, of the tribe of Benjamin, a Hebrew of Hebrews; in regard to the law, a Pharisee; as for zeal, persecuting the church; as for righteousness based on the law, faultless. But whatever were gains to me I now consider loss for the sake of Christ. What is more, I consider everything a loss because of the surpassing worth of knowing Christ Jesus my Lord, for whose sake I have lost all things. I consider them garbage, that I may gain Christ and be found in him, not having a righteousness of my own that comes from the law, but that which is through faith in Christ—the righteousness that comes from God on the basis of faith.

Notice that Paul says directly, "in regard to the law, a Pharisee . . . as for righteousness based on the law, faultless." Yet Paul puts all of this aside and considers it garbage! True righteousness comes through faith in Jesus Christ. That does not mean, however, that Christians are allowed to become lawless. It is important to understand that faith itself calls us to a new ethic that indeed *"surpasses* that of the Pharisees" (Matthew 5:20). It is an ethic based on holy love.

So what did Jesus mean by "the Law and Prophets"? Put simply, Jesus was making a statement that Christians were not to set aside the Old Testament and Jewish history! There was a heretic in the early period of the church who wanted to do exactly that. His name was Marcion, and he believed that the God of the Israelites was a different God altogether than the God of Jesus. He cut everything out of the New Testament that made reference to the Old Testament. In the end, he had little left! Jesus did not come as a Savior who was disconnected from the entire story of Israel and its anticipation of the Messiah. Instead, Jesus came to *fulfill* Israel's hope! The Old Testament is not lesser than the New. We should see the relationship as promise, then fulfillment. It is appropriate for Christians to read the Old Testament as deeply and necessarily connected to the New.

A Higher Standard

You have heard that it was said to the people long ago, "You shall not murder, and anyone who murders will be subject to judgment." But I tell you that anyone who is angry with a brother or sister will be subject to judgment. Again, anyone who says to a brother or sister, "Raca," is answerable to the court. And anyone who says, "You fool!" will be in danger of the fire of hell.

Therefore, if you are offering your gift at the altar and there remember that your brother or sister has something against you, leave your gift there in front of the altar. First go and be reconciled to them; then come and offer your gift.

Settle matters quickly with your adversary who is taking you to court. Do it while you are still together on the way, or your adversary may hand you over to the judge, and the judge may hand you over to the officer, and you may be thrown into prison. Truly I tell you, you will not get out until you have paid the last penny.

—Matthew 5:21–26

What we see in these verses is how this righteousness that surpasses the Pharisees—who were the exacting keepers of the law—plays itself out in real-life relationships. What Jesus teaches here will play out in his own ministry. Laws are misused if they end up hurting people. For example, the Pharisees accused Jesus of wrongdoing when he healed a person on the Sabbath. Obviously Jesus valued the person above a strict rendering of the commandment.

Jesus implied in these verses that we are to live to an even higher standard than the law. He said, *You have heard, "do not murder," but I tell you, do not even be angry.* The point here was not to make a new law out of the prohibition of anger! (Did anyone else hear growing up that Christians should never be angry but should praise God when they hit their thumb with a hammer?) Rather, Jesus pointed out practical situations where anger went too far. Anger tends to hurt others, and it hurts the relationship between ourselves and our friends or even our adversaries. Overall, Jesus admonished his hearers to live in relationships of reconciliation, kindness, and love. This very high standard was demonstrated by Jesus's strong words that merely calling someone a fool would place us in danger of the fires of hell.

Our Bodies Matter

You have heard that it was said, "You shall not commit adultery." But I tell you that anyone who looks at a woman lustfully has

What we do with our bodies matters.

*already committed adultery with her in his heart. If your right eye
causes you to stumble, gouge it out and throw it away. It is better
for you to lose one part of your body than for your whole body to
be thrown into hell. And if your right hand causes you to stumble,
cut it off and throw it away. It is better for you to lose one part of
your body than for your whole body to go into hell.*

*It has been said, "Anyone who divorces his wife must give her
a certificate of divorce." But I tell you that anyone who divorces
his wife, except for sexual immorality, makes her the victim of
adultery, and anyone who marries a divorced woman commits
adultery.*

—*Matthew 5:27–32*

Verses 29 and 30 are verses we would do well *not* to
take literally! And, of course, we haven't, or else churches might be full of one-eyed, one-handed people. But we
should hear this literally: *what we do with our bodies matters.*
Gnosticism was a widespread and dangerous heresy in the
early years of Christianity that misinterpreted the gospel in
many significant ways, including dismissing the Old Testament. Another aspect of Gnostic philosophy was the idea
that what really matters most is our spirit, which Gnostic adherents saw as disconnected from our bodies. They
actually thought that what we do with our bodies wouldn't
affect our spirituality or our faith.

The New Testament is clear that we are to view ourselves and our faith as holistic—body and spirit are deeply
connected. Sections of Paul's writings that are devoted to
warnings about sexual immorality indicate this connection
clearly:

Do you not know that your bodies are members of
Christ himself? Shall I then take the members of
Christ and unite them with a prostitute? Never!
(1 Corinthians 6:15)

Flee from sexual immorality. . . . Do you not know
that your bodies are temples of the Holy Spirit, who
is in you, whom you have received from God? You are
not your own.
(1 Corinthians 6:18a, 19)

Our bodies matter.

Jesus's words help us regard both body and spirit as
important, directing our attention beyond the external acts
to the internal offense. Jesus was clear that yes, what we do
with our bodies does matter, but we can also sin against
another person in the privacy of our own hearts. In the case
of murder and adultery, Jesus was obviously quoting from
the Ten Commandments. What is perhaps less obvious is
that Jesus's words about lust can also be connected to the
Ten Commandments "You shall not covet your neighbor's
wife" (Exodus 20:17).

This command helps us define lust. Lust should not
be equated with normal sexual attraction and feelings. We
have damaged too many of our teens and young people by
shaming them for their natural sexual feelings and impulses.
When Jesus used the words "anyone who looks at a woman,"
he was implying more than seeing, even more than mere
attraction. This phrase means *leering* to the point that the
person has become an *object* of our desire, which means we
have lost control to the point of coveting. Lust is entertain-
ing a desire to the point of dehumanizing the person we see,
disrespecting them, objectifying them, reducing them to
nothing more than a source of our own gratification.

It is appropriate for Jesus to move straight from lust to
divorce because these are relational sins. Leering at a person
to the point that we dehumanize and objectify them and
divorcing a spouse in a trivial and unloving manner are relational sins. Because of the brokenness of our world, we often experience brokenness in our relationships, even in the
church, and even in Christian marriages. In this passage of

Scripture, Jesus was addressing a real problem in his own culture, even among Jewish leaders. Based on a loophole in the law that was being exploited, men were divorcing their wives, sometimes multiple times, for the equivalent of burning dinner. In this context, it was important for Jesus to limit the right to divorce to marital infidelity.

Divorce was being treated lightly, and Jesus was adamant that it should not be. Since women in that culture did not work and there was no type of welfare or social security, divorced women were often stigmatized even by their own families, often to the point that the *only* way divorced women had to survive was to turn to prostitution. Although the consequences of divorce in modern culture are not usually quite as dramatic, there is often still a traumatic aftermath for those whose marriages end, especially in situations where adultery or domestic abuse have been involved.

What should the church's stance be on divorce today then? We should do all we can to work toward reconciliation *where it is appropriate*—but there are times when reconciliation is not appropriate. When divorce happens, our responsibility is to be redemptive and loving toward those who have suffered from its destructive force. After all, divorce is not the unpardonable sin. For too long we in the church have looked at and treated divorced people as "less than." This value judgment is simply not true in God's eyes. God is always a redemptive God who can touch even our most difficult experiences with Christ's new creation.

Our relationships matter. Relationships are central to any sufficient treatment of holiness, for holiness is not a theology, however good it might be. Holiness is lived life in a world of infinite relationships. We cannot be holy in isolation. We might even say that with great power—the power of holiness enabled by the Spirit—comes great responsibility, toward others particularly. This is the very highest standard of holy living.

.

THREE

Love without Limits

Is living a holy life really possible? Yes! But it is crucial for us to understand that we cannot be holy if we are only attempting to live up to some external code of conduct. Striving for holiness without an *internal* change in our motivations and our character—and without grace—will cause us to fail quite miserably.

Holiness as Integrity

Holiness is more than an ideal to strive for, more than straining to change our behavior through a sheer act of our own will. The Wesleyan-Holiness tradition lost its way for a time when the vibrancy of life in the Spirit was reduced to stagnant legalism. We never lost the goal of the holy life, but we failed to always make clear *how* the holy life is lived. As a result, holiness during this era was motivated by duty and equated with a set of behaviors that too often emphasized what we should *not* do, rather than what we *do* do through the life of love. This misstep led to equating prescribed moral codes with personal holiness, which in reality neglected the very core of the Wesleyan message of holiness of heart and life.

During this present age of moral ambiguity, there is a great need to get to the heart of the matter. We need to examine not only the standards and behaviors of holy living but also the internal motivation for such living. If the internal motivation remains listless obligation, the lifeblood of holiness will be sucked out of holiness theology, leaving it anemic and on the verge of death. It is absolutely crucial that we return to Wesley's own emphasis on holy *character* and how it is developed. We act out of a right heart—and our heart is only made right through the sanctifying grace of God. Sanctifying grace—given in important ways through attending to spiritual practices every day, and given in a deeply significant way in the experience of entire sanctification—is the very means by which our character is changed, and the only way we will ever be able to live a holy life.

Holy people are people of integrity. Integrity has sometimes been described as *doing what is right when no one is looking*. It is the opposite of hypocrisy. What we do on the outside matches who we are on the inside. Our actions flow out of our character. Jesus criticized the Pharisees the most for appearing clean on the outside when their hearts were anything but. They might appear to obey the law, but they did it for the wrong reasons. Jesus emphasized a quality of heart that surpasses sheer adherence to rules. Indeed, love both supersedes *and* fulfills the law!

As we work through the next biblical text in the Sermon on the Mount, it should become clear that the life Jesus calls us to requires that we be transformed from the inside out.

Love as Honesty

Again, you have heard that it was said to the people long ago, "Do not break your oath, but fulfill to the Lord the vows you have made." But I tell you, do not swear an oath at all: either by heaven, for it is God's throne; or by the earth, for it is his footstool; or by Jerusalem, for it is the city of the Great King. And do not swear by your head, for you cannot make even one hair white or black. All you need to say is simply "Yes" or "No"; anything beyond this comes from the evil one.

—Matthew 5:33–37

Sanctifying grace is the very means
by which our character is changed, and the only
way we will ever be able to live a holy life.

Jesus continued the "you have heard . . . but I tell you" pattern, this time about the practice of making oaths. What is wrong with making oaths? Or, to use today's language, what's wrong with saying, "I swear" to get the point across that we are really telling the truth? In Jesus's day, apparently the degree of honesty was based on a scale of what was invoked to swear by. They would swear by heaven, or earth, or Jerusalem, or their own heads. They would not dare to swear by God, so they used substitute words.

Today, we quite easily say, "I swear to God" with no regard to the reverence that should be given to God's name. This certainly should not be done. Yet if we turn "do not swear" into an external law to follow, we have again missed Christ's point. The need to swear in such a binding way suggests that a person has lied in the past and therefore may not be altogether dependable. Lying makes us people without integrity, people of dubious character, people who live by double standards who have to appeal to something other than our own word to prove our trustworthiness. Jesus's words are clear: the need to swear to make up for previous lies comes from an evil heart.

Love as Generosity

You have heard that it was said, "Eye for eye, and tooth for tooth." But I tell you, do not resist an evil person. If anyone slaps you on the right cheek, turn to them the other cheek also. And if anyone wants to sue you and take your shirt, hand over your coat as well. If anyone forces you to go one mile, go with them two miles. Give to the one who asks you, and do not turn away from the one who wants to borrow from you.

—Matthew 5:38–42

The "eye for eye" section also focuses on the condition of the heart. The Jewish law spoke of a kind of justice that kept people from escalating the degree of harm to someone who wronged them. This law's very existence clearly speaks of the corruption of the human heart: we are prone to hateful anger, to righteous indignation, and to shameless desire for revenge when we are hurt or offended. Interestingly, the law allowed for some measure of revenge. The purpose of the law was not to *encourage* revenge but to *limit* how vengeful the people were allowed to be.

But Jesus stood the law on its head, emphasizing not only that we should not seek revenge but also that we are to treat others *better* than how they have treated us. Without the grace of God that transforms our hearts, such a disposition would be impossible. When we are slapped, our inclination is to slap back. If someone takes our shirt, we snatch it back—and possibly take something of theirs in return. When we are obligated to do something for another person, we may be willing to do what we have to, but often we refuse to go an inch more. If someone borrows something from us, we meticulously keep score. It requires a very different kind of inner character to give willingly and generously, particularly when we have been offended. Jesus again raised the standard even above the law.

Love toward All

You have heard that it was said, "Love your neighbor and hate your enemy." But I tell you, love your enemies and pray for those who persecute you, that you may be children of your Father in heaven. He causes his sun to rise on the evil and the good, and sends rain on the righteous and the unrighteous. If you love those who love you, what reward will you get? Are not even the tax collectors doing that? And if you greet only your own people, what are you doing more than others? Do not even pagans do that? Be perfect, therefore, as your heavenly Father is perfect.

—Matthew 5:43–48

God seeks to transform our very nature
so that love best describes us.

The previous passage taught about something very difficult—giving willingly and generously when we have been offended. Without even giving us time to acclimate to that difficult teaching, Jesus extended the mandate in the very next passage to include people who simply do not deserve it. If there is anything that speaks to the upside-down nature of God's kingdom, it is the revolutionary command of Jesus to love our enemies. It is just as outrageous as the command, a few verses later, to be perfect. We cannot act lovingly toward our enemies—let alone always consistently love those we care about—unless we are a loving person *by nature*. With our corrupted natures, is there any hope?

Yes, the hope of the gospel is that God forgives our sins, but we believe even more than that. God seeks to transform our very nature so that love best describes us. What God *calls* us to be, God *enables* us to be through the Holy Spirit. Rather than trying to repress our sins, or trying to rise above our sin through our own efforts, God's presence is more powerful than the power of sin; and that presence changes us into persons who are able to love from pure hearts. Our full surrender is also required to allow God's grace to work and transform us. God is not stingy with grace—quite the opposite. But we can block our ability to receive grace through our lack of full commitment, and our resistance to practice the virtue God wants to instill in us.

As we consecrate ourselves, and as we practice love in cooperation with the Holy Spirit in us, our capacity to love grows so that we can really say we are a people with a truly loving character, out of which true love flows—even to those who do not deserve it. Just as we were once enemies of God and are now reconciled through love, so too does God enable us to love even our enemies. God created us for the purpose of loving God and loving others with our whole being and from a pure heart. Our hearts are purified through the holy presence of God within us. When we express this love, we fulfill our purpose and are thus expressing "Christian perfection."

We do not claim Christian perfection as a type of accomplishment or spiritual stature. We don't even claim we have been sanctified with any sort of pride or superiority. We are completely dependent on God for any progress in holiness.

FOUR

The Outflow of a Holy Heart

Holiness as Humility

Humility is a disposition of the heart. The term "humility" comes from the Latin word *humilitas*, which means having the characteristic of being humble. It can also be translated as "grounded" or "from the earth," since it derives from *humus*, which means "earth." We are made from the dust of the earth and, as such, cannot rival God. Humility is absolutely essential to holiness, and speaks of our need to ascribe divine worth only to God. Only God is to be worshiped. Pride—the opposite of humility—can be called idolatry of the self. Holiness, on the other hand, is built on a willing surrender of the whole self and an appropriate yielding to God's will and way in our lives. Holiness and humility are intricately connected.

Unfortunately, we sometimes take humility too far. There is an appropriate level of esteem we should hold for ourselves as persons who are created and renewed in the image of God. An overemphasis on humility can take us to a place of unhealthy self-deprecation, where our own feelings of self-hatred interfere with what God wants to do in us. Just as Jesus uses the word "hate" (see Luke 14:26) as a *contrast* to the degree of loyalty and love we are to give to God alone (and thus does not mean it to be taken literally), so too self-hate is not to be taken literally as a Christian virtue. We are to have a correct evaluation of our worth based on the redemption God has provided to us out of infinite love. Humility that goes too far is unhealthy for us and often toxic to those around us.

The danger of false humility also arises in this discussion. True humility is distinct from false humility, which consists of deprecating one's gifts, talents, and accomplishments for the express purpose of receiving praise and adulation from others. Jesus calls false humility into question, indicting all who would hypocritically flaunt their own self-righteousness in a false form of spiritual humility so they can receive accolades.

As with the entire Sermon on the Mount, Jesus continued in Matthew 6 to emphasize that our motivations matter just as much as our actions. Indeed, later Jesus clearly said that right actions come from a right heart and evil actions from an evil heart (see Matthew 7:18; 15:18–19; 23:25–26). Jesus was deeply concerned about the public practices of the Pharisees in particular. Any disciple can fall into the trap of doing the right things for the wrong reasons. Spiritual pride is a real and present danger.

The Right Spirit of Charity

Be careful not to practice your righteousness in front of others to be seen by them. If you do, you will have no reward from your Father in heaven.

So when you give to the needy, do not announce it with trumpets, as the hypocrites do in the synagogues and on the streets, to be honored by others. Truly I tell you, they have received their reward in full. But when you give to the needy, do not let your left hand know what your right hand is doing, so that your giving may be in secret. Then your Father, who sees what is done in secret, will reward you.

—Matthew 6:1–4

Are we trying to impress people with our holiness?
Or are we obeying God with a simplicity of trust
that comes out of appropriate humility?

Jesus maintained his focus but also began a new pattern in this passage, contrasting acting for show with acting humbly for God alone. The haughty might get some attention here and now, but that is the extent of their reward. The humble, on the other hand, will receive rewards that matter in God's eternal kingdom.

The first topic Jesus addressed was acts of charity. We can give to the needy so that others see how righteous we are, or we can give in such a way that no one sees our generosity but God. Jesus went so far as to call those who give to the needy in a public manner "hypocrites"—perhaps because people who need to publicize their good deeds usually have something else to hide. The other extreme is the person who acts seemingly almost unconsciously out of a pure heart—to the point of not letting the left hand know what the right hand is doing. Of course, it is objectively good for the needy to be helped, regardless of the manner in which we give. But those doing the giving should examine their motives carefully, for God sees their hearts and judges accordingly.

The Right Posture for Prayer

And when you pray, do not be like the hypocrites, for they love to pray standing in the synagogues and on the street corners to be seen by others. Truly I tell you, they have received their reward in full. But when you pray, go into your room, close the door and pray to your Father, who is unseen. Then your Father, who sees what is done in secret, will reward you. And when you pray, do not keep on babbling like pagans, for they think they will be heard because of their many words. Do not be like them, for your Father knows what you need before you ask him.

This, then, is how you should pray:

"Our Father in heaven,
hallowed be your name,

your kingdom come,
your will be done,
on earth as it is in heaven.
Give us today our daily bread.
And forgive us our debts,
as we also have forgiven our debtors.
And lead us not into temptation,
but deliver us from the evil one."

For if you forgive other people when they sin against you, your
heavenly Father will also forgive you. But if you do not forgive
others their sins, your Father will not forgive your sins.

—Matthew 6:5–15

Most of us know the Lord's Prayer, but we sometimes forget the context in which Jesus first said it. Here it is set in a context where Jesus offered not so much a *teaching* on how to pray, as compared to Luke 11:2–4, for example. Instead, the emphasis in Matthew is on the right *attitude* in which to pray. Jesus's focus was on the humility of our hearts when praying—in direct contrast to the pride and hypocrisy of his contemporary religious leaders. We do not pray for show. We do not pray eloquently so everyone will think we are really spiritual and righteous. The best way to avoid trying to impress people is to pray in private, in a closet, Jesus said, so no one can hear us but God.

These verses make another important point encompassed in verse 7: "do not keep on babbling like pagans." God knows what we need. Jesus was referring to those who babbled and rambled on pointlessly, heaping up empty phrases. The word in Greek used here and translated as "babble" is not used elsewhere in the New Testament, so a bit of translation needs to be done. In that day, pagans believed there were many gods. One thing they did when praying was rattle off the names of all the gods they could think of, believing if they came upon the right name, that god would listen to them and answer their requests. Commentators also mention that they believed they could get their prayers answered by overwhelming the gods with flattery. It was a way of trying to control the gods by pestering them.

Another form of pagan prayer was the attempt to appease the gods in order to keep their anger away. Pagans thought that if they pleased the gods enough, by saying *enough* words and the *right* words, and if they appeased the anger of the gods by using flattery and smooth talking, they would be kept from calamity and all would be well; they would be healthy and wealthy, and all would be peaceful—until the next day, when the prayers had to be said all over again.

Jesus said, *don't do that.* Jesus was talking about more than just babbling. He was also talking about the ideas we might have about God that would make us sound an awful lot like pagans:

1. We might assume God can be manipulated. If we can just get the formula down—say the right words in the right way—we can get what we want. Jesus said no.
2. We might assume God's anger needs to be appeased. Maybe God is looking for every opportunity to punish us, just waiting for us to mess up. Jesus said no.
3. We might assume we must beg and beg and beg God for what we need—as if God doesn't already know what we need. Jesus said no to that too.

There are still other twisted beliefs about God that might make us sound like pagans—more subtle and more dangerous yet widely held by a vast number of evangelical Christians.

One such idea suggests that if I have a good life, that means God is pleased with me. I must be doing something right.

Even more subtle and more dangerous is the idea that if someone else has a good life, God has blessed them, and they are the ones we should follow, emulate, and imitate because they're doing it right.

Most dangerous of all is the idea that if someone else has hard circumstances in their life, it is a sign of God's judgment, and we should avoid those people because they're doing it wrong.

The problem with subtleties is that sometimes we hardly notice we are buying into them. That is why Jesus had to tell us not to believe what the pagans believe. But he didn't stop there. In verse 8, Jesus gave a very different perspective on who God really is, assuring us that God knows what we need before we even ask—which implies that this God knows us intimately. This God is trustworthy, compassionate, loving, and good—and this God knows what we need. *God is trustworthy.* This is not something we should affirm flippantly. It is a statement of deep faith to proclaim God as faithful. God's economy is not like ours, not based on matching blessings or curses with good or bad behavior. God is a God of grace, and grace makes no sense from a pagan perspective because it is based on the nature and character of *God*, not our own.

The Right Mindset for Fasting

When you fast, do not look somber as the hypocrites do, for they disfigure their faces to show others they are fasting. Truly I tell you, they have received their reward in full. But when you fast, put oil on your head and wash your face, so that it will not be obvious to others that you are fasting, but only to your Father, who is unseen; and your Father, who sees what is done in secret, will reward you.

—*Matthew 6:16–18*

Jesus and his own disciples were criticized for not fasting more, to which Jesus replied that they would have plenty of time to fast once he was gone (see Mark 2:18–20). Fasting was a biweekly observance ingrained in Hebrew practice. The Pharisees, as with everything else, followed fasting practices strictly, which is why they criticized Jesus.

The reason for and meaning of fasting has an interesting history in the Christian church. God's people have indeed fasted—from the ascetic practices of early monks and nuns up until today. Interestingly, though, the reason for Christian fasting has taken a different turn through the centuries from what fasting meant in the Bible. Today we practice what can be called "instrumental fasting." This is the teaching that asserts that we fast in order to receive something from God, or to gain some benefit. Whether that benefit is spiritual growth, the ability to handle temptation, the hope of answered prayer, or clarity of insight, modern Christian fasting has tended to focus on what *we* acquire from the practice.

In the Old Testament, however, fasting is a response to God in light of crises like death, war, a sin, and God's judgment. Fasting was done in the same spirit as rending one's clothes, or putting on sackcloth and ashes. Fasting was associated with repentance. So there is great irony in these verses because Jesus was highlighting the tendency to be proud and showy even about one's own repentance. We should not be like the hypocrites who look somber, disfigure their faces, and make their fasting evident to all. Those who want to be true disciples fast for God alone. Jesus indicated there will be a greater reward for those who act out of humble hearts, those who are not fasting to manipulate God, those who are not trying to impress others by their devotion.

There is a holy attitude that must accompany what are called holy acts. It is not enough to give to the poor, to pray, or to fast if our motives are wrong. Christ points us again and again to the fact that God looks at the heart. Are we trying to impress people with our holiness? Or are we obeying God with a simplicity of trust that comes out of appropriate humility? God will not be fooled, even if we fool others— even if we fool ourselves. But here is the good news: anyone can be changed by grace into a truly humble and loving person! We dare to believe that the God who forgives our sin is the same God who can change our nature into genuine Christlikeness as we mature. Thanks be to God.

The Journey of Sanctification and Wholeness

FIVE

Holiness Gone Wrong

This is the message we have heard from him and declare to you: God is light; in him there is no darkness at all. If we claim to have fellowship with him and yet walk in the darkness, we lie and do not live out the truth. But if we walk in the light, as he is in the light, we have fellowship with one another, and the blood of Jesus, his Son, purifies us from all sin.

If we claim to be without sin, we deceive ourselves and the truth is not in us. If we confess our sins, he is faithful and just and will forgive us our sins and purify us from all unrighteousness. If we claim we have not sinned, we make him out to be a liar and his word is not in us.

My dear children, I write this to you so that you will not sin. But if anybody does sin, we have an advocate with the Father—Jesus Christ, the Righteous One. He is the atoning sacrifice for our sins, and not only for ours but also for the sins of the whole world.

—1 John 1:5–2:2

We return to a paradox. Here in 1 John we find the paradox of the expectation that we do not sin right alongside the admission that we *do* sin and need forgiveness and Christ's advocacy. John writes so we will not sin; we are purified from all sin and unrighteousness—yet we should not claim we are sinless, and we rely on Christ's atoning sacrifice. A really important question is how the Wesleyan-Holiness tradition has handled this paradox.

If theology is primarily about God and God's relationship with humanity, then any full-orbed discussion of a theology of holiness must pay attention to the significant break of relationship between God and humans—namely, sin. Likewise, if a theology of holiness is the main emphasis of Wesleyan-Holiness theology and the goal of Christian life and practice, sin must also be thoroughly considered as the greatest threat to holiness. Sin is not just an abstract theory or theology; it is lived out in real life, where it hurts, destroys, and harms not only others but ourselves as well. Sin keeps us from the holy, loving living we were created for.

While there was much theology formed very early in church history, sin took longer to define; it does not show up in the ecumenical councils or creeds, except in the phrase "I believe in the forgiveness of sin." Even today there are various interpretations of what sin is. There are differences between theological traditions when answering questions such as the following:

What is at the heart of sin?

Are there different categories of sin?

What is original sin, or inherited depravity?

Is sin inevitable?

How does the work of Christ and the work of the Holy Spirit affect sin, and what can we hope for in this life?

The following pages can only serve as an introduction to this complex topic, yet we will attempt to gain more clarity about sin, for if we lack clarity on sin, we can also misunderstand salvation, sanctification, the church, and the mission of God in the world—all connected to the meaning and purpose of the Christian life as love, and all threatened by the destructive nature of sin.

The first thing that needs to be said is that the doctrine of sin, called *hamartiology*, divides sin into three main categories: 1) personal sin, 2) original sin, and 3) systemic evil. The first two will be addressed in this chapter.

Personal Sin

"Personal sin" refers to sinful acts done by individuals. There are many ways to define personal sin. The original Greek word *hamartia* literally means to miss the mark, as when aiming at a target. Some have simply called sin disobedience against God. For others, it is falling short of the glory of God; for still more, it is the willful transgression of a known law of God.

One of the key issues that actually separates different theological traditions is the question of whether sin properly defined must always be intentional, or volitional. One particular tradition's perspective defines sin more broadly than the Wesleyan-Holiness tradition does. For John Calvin, sin does *not* have to be a willful act; the category of sin, for Calvin, also includes the multiple ways we fall short of God's intentions, such as our lack of wisdom, our poor choices, our mistakes, and all our imperfections that are common to being human. Calvin's understanding of sin was very wide. It is no wonder, then, that he implied sin was inevitable and would persist throughout the whole Christian life—he was working with a different definition of sin. The question of sin is a key doctrine on which Wesleyans and Calvinists disagree. Although Wesleyans can sometimes define sin too narrowly, in general we do affirm that a person is aware of their own sin. Sin is a willful act in the Wesleyan theological paradigm.

When Wesley considers such realities as imperfections, or what he calls "infirmities," he believes these to be amoral—behaviors that are neither moral nor immoral. It is possible for our actions to be amoral in that they may fall short of absolute human perfection, but God does not hold us morally responsible for such limitations. Rather, God holds us accountable only when we choose to participate in sin—when we give in to temptation and harm our relationship with God or others *willingly*.

When we examine the Ten Commandments
and all the laws given by God, we discover
that each one is *relational*!
Each commandment prohibits
an action that goes against love.

Affirming a willful doctrine of sin does not mean we are not still responsible to one another when we harm others unintentionally. When we hurt someone unknowingly, and they point it out to us, our response should not be, "I'm not responsible because I didn't mean it!" Our love and commitments to one another should surely lead us to genuine sorrow and apologies, despite the innocence of our intent. In a similar way, even though God might not hold us eternally accountable for unintentional acts, the same sorrow and confession should be our loving response to God when we discover we have inadvertently missed the mark. Such love and responsiveness are at the heart of every relationship, especially when damage is done. In relationship, we commit ourselves to improve and grow.

Wesley labeled imperfections, infirmities and unintentional failures as "sin improperly so called." When Wesleyans exclude these from a definition of sin, it makes much more sense when we affirm that sin is *not* inevitable, necessary, or perpetual in the Christian life. We believe that grace—forgiving and sanctifying grace—is greater than the power of sin! "Sin properly so called" implies willfulness, yet the Holy Spirit can help us be victorious over such willfulness as we grow in our sanctification, character, and love.

When we do deliberately break the laws of God—those specified and written down, and those written upon our hearts—we sin. Such sins are further categorized as sins of *commission*. When we break the laws of God or the law of love, we commit sin.

There are also sins of *omission*. James makes this type of sin very clear: "If anyone, then, knows the good they ought to do and doesn't do it, it is sin for them" (4:17). James addresses several problematic issues in his short epistle. For instance, his original audience consisted of people who were showing favoritism toward the rich and neglecting the poor. They knew the right and good thing was to feed the hungry and lift up the oppressed, and they chose not to do it. They *omitted* the good—and therefore sinned.

Sins of omission demonstrate an important reason to live confessional lives before God. There is need all around us. It is impossible for us to spend every moment fulfilling the needs of the whole world. But we do need to be in tune with the Holy Spirit in order to be led to specific situations where God wants us to intervene. When we don't obey in those instances, according to James, we sin and need to confess. It is obviously impossible to address every need in every moment. We will fall short. We will sin by omission. Acknowledging this reality should bring us humbly before the throne of grace, even if we never committed a "thou shalt not." We pray the Lord's Prayer and do not neglect "forgive us our trespasses."

Another aspect of the doctrine of sin is to ask an essential question about personal sin, whether sins of commission or omission: *How do we know sin when we see it?* Is there a way to identify sin? What is at the *essence* of sin? Let's think about the Ten Commandments for a moment. It is easy to think of them as arbitrary, believing that God randomly chose ten specific things to prohibit so that humans would know when they had displeased God, and so they would always remember that God is God and they are not. If this is how we view the Ten Commandments, we might imagine that one of the ten could've just as easily been, "Thou shalt not wear purple socks." From that perspective, the only way to determine what sin is would be to memorize all the 613 prohibitions of Mosaic law, as the Pharisees did.

In reality, when we examine the Ten Commandments and all the laws given by God, we discover that each one is *relational*! Each commandment prohibits an action that goes against love. When we worship other gods or graven images, we cease to love God, turning toward inadequate idols that can never satisfy us. When we steal, or murder, or bear false witness, we cease to love one another.

This perspective on the Ten Commandments is why Jesus said we fulfill the whole law when we truly love God with all of our being and love our neighbors as ourselves (see Matthew 22:34–40; Mark 12:28–31). It also explains why Jesus said our righteousness must exceed the righteousness of the Pharisees (Matthew 5:20). The Pharisees may have obeyed the 613 law, but they missed the point of love. Indeed, to really love as God desires, our love must go beyond a legalistic understanding of law as determining right and wrong. *Love* is the measure of our Christian ethic, so when we come across situations where there is no law, we can still discern the right course of action if we pursue true *agape* love.

Sin, at its essence, is anti-love. Love, at its essence, leaves no room for sin. That is why Wesley said that love excludes sin. If the heart is filled with love, there will no longer be room for sin. The contrary image of a heart filled with sin brings us to the discussion of original sin.

Original Sin

Before the year 386, the theology of sin focused almost exclusively on personal sin, emphasizing freedom of will. After 386, one of Christianity's greatest converts, Augustine, developed ideas about *why* we sin in the first place. Augustine interpreted the Genesis scene in the garden, reflecting on the fall and the origin of sin entering the pristine world God created. He also reflected on his own life and struggle with sin, identifying with Paul's writings in Romans 7, where he describes sin acting like a master over him before he met Christ. Augustine's thoughts were also formed by encountering the writings of a British monk named Pelagius. For Pelagius, the only effect of the fall on the future of humanity was that it brought mortality to humans. The sin of Adam and Eve caused death to enter the world so that every human being thereafter would die. Pelagius was concerned that if a doctrine of original sin were pushed too far, there would be no way for individuals to be held accountable for their sins.

Augustine believed there were more consequences from the fall than mere mortality. He began to argue that all generations after Adam and Eve would inherit a sinful disposition. This inherited depravity affects every human being ever born (except Jesus). Therefore, when Augustine pondered the question of why we sin, he concluded that humans sin because we are born with a sinful nature. Free will is, in a sense, lost. We are only free to sin, according to Augustine. These ideas came to be known as the doctrine of original sin. The doctrine was affirmed, and Pelagius determined a heretic, at the Council of Orange in the year 529, although the council did not affirm everything Augustine believed (such as his strong view of predestination).

John Wesley believed in original sin but did not agree entirely with Augustine. Besides rejecting predestination, Wesley added his doctrine of prevenient grace to the prevailing understanding of original sin. Prevenient grace has many functions in the world, including the belief that the Holy Spirit is at work in every person's life by drawing, or "wooing," them into relationship with God. Wesley also used prevenient grace to explain that, even though everybody is born with original sin, we are also given a grace that restores our free will. This caveat was important for Wesley because, without a graciously restored free will, no one could be justly held accountable for sin (which would give credence to predestination). If original sin compels one to sin against their will, how would God be just in holding them accountable for sinning, if they are only doing something they cannot help but do? Prevenient grace allows us to answer this question. Although Wesley held strongly to a doctrine of free grace from the moment we are born, he also affirmed that we continue to be influenced toward sin by reigning sin, even in the Christian life. "Reigning sin" was his preferred term instead of original sin.

The idea of reigning sin becomes important in Wesley's discussion of holiness and sanctification. In disagreement with his Moravian friends, Wesley finally concluded that people are not entirely sanctified at the moment they convert to Christ. Even though all *sins* are forgiven by the atoning grace of God received at the new birth, the sinful disposition remains, and can even *reign* in the Christian life. God's sanctifying presence is the only thing that can replace sin in a Christian's heart with love. To be entirely sanctified is to allow love to *reign* so that love might exclude sin.

Does sanctifying grace make it impossible for Christians to sin after they are entirely sanctified? In his mature theology, Wesley came to believe that sanctified Christians could certainly sin! To believe otherwise would be to place ourselves above Christ, for we must maintain that Christ was truly tempted and was truly *able* to sin. More to the point, Wesley ultimately concluded that absolute sinlessness is not possible in this life, particularly due to sins of omission. Yet he also affirmed that our disposition and our character can be so radically changed by God's holy presence that we sin less and *want* to sin less the more we abide in Christ.

Holiness should not be equated with sinlessness. We should not define holiness by using the absence of sin. I could be sinless and still not be holy because holiness must have a positive content—holiness must be defined as the *presence* of perfect love, of God-given, divine *agape*, not as the absence of sin. I may avoid sin altogether, but if I have not love, I am nothing (see 1 Corinthians 13:1–3). Even stronger, to relate to others without love is to sin. Sin is anti-love.

If we go back to Augustine, we will find that, for him, the very essence of sin is pride. Much of Western Christianity adopted this definition, but Wesley was more nuanced. Wesley often defined the essence of sin as *idolatry*. Examine the chart provided.

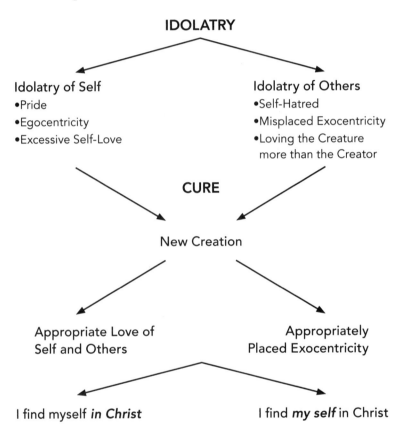

IDOLATRY

Idolatry of Self
•Pride
•Egocentricity
•Excessive Self-Love

Idolatry of Others
•Self-Hatred
•Misplaced Exocentricity
•Loving the Creature more than the Creator

CURE

New Creation

Appropriate Love of Self and Others

Appropriately Placed Exocentricity

I find myself *in Christ*

I find *my self* in Christ

For Wesley, sin is idolatry. Idolatry can express itself in two ways. On the left side of the chart, we see a well-known description. Sin has often been portrayed as pride, egocentricity, or excessive self-love. These are ways to describe an idolatry of *self*. Those who are egocentric destroy relationships through their own self-absorption.

Scholars of Wesley, and even of the early church, recognize another way to express sin as seen in Christian history.[1] There is an expression of sin that opposes the words on the left. On the right-hand side of the chart, we recognize that idolatry of others can also dominate a heart of sin. "Loving the creature more than the Creator" is a biblical idea (see Romans 1:25) that Wesley often employed. If egocentricity is a form of sin, then its foil is misplaced exocentricity ("exo" meaning outside oneself)—which means to find oneself only in the love of another human being (or in drugs, money, power, and so on). This type of sin causes a person to be completely dependent on others for their identity, which leads to self-hatred and also destroys relationships. Self-loathing is not God's intent for humanity. Sometimes we get humility and self-hatred mixed up. God want us to be humble—but only after God empowers us to *have a self* that we then can give up in love.

As the chart shows, the cure for both idolatry of self and idolatry of others is Christ alone. In Christ, we are created anew. We find our identity in Christ's love and sacrifice for us. Our exocentricity or egocentricity become *appropriately* placed in God, rather than in others or ourselves. As God writes God's name on our hearts, and as we allow God to reign in our lives, then we are able to love ourselves and others appropriately. We find ourselves in Christ. For some, finding themselves *in Christ* is emphasized as they reorient their egocentric selves toward God. For those on the right, *finding themselves* in Christ is emphasized as they experience the very birth of a self that God has loved.

Sin is anti-love that damages, even devastates, relationships. Personal sins—whether of commission or omis-

---

1. See Diane Leclerc, *Singleness of Heart: Gender, Sin, and Holiness in Historical Perspective* (Lanham, MD: Scarecrow Press, 2001) for historical figures whose work contributed to this view, including Jerome, Chrystosom, John Wesley, Phoebe Palmer, and Søren Kierkegaard.

sion—keep us from being all that God has created us to be as individuals and in relationship with God and others. God hates sin because it destroys us, whom God loves. We also affirm that beneath our personal sins is original, or reigning, sin as an influence that damages the image of God within us. Through new birth and sanctification, we can live into the love of God that dwells within us as God restores our original image. We do not have to live in bondage to sin our entire earthly lives. Wesleyan optimism is founded on the incredible grace of God that changes and transforms us from the inside out as we participate with the Holy Spirit in order to be and live like Jesus.

SIX

Sanctifying Grace

It is God's will that you should be sanctified.

—1 Thessalonians 4:3a

May God himself, the God of peace, sanctify you through and through.
May your whole spirit, soul and body be kept blameless at the coming of
our Lord Jesus Christ. The one who calls you is faithful, and he will do it.
—1 Thessalonians 5:23–24

What Is Sanctification?

The word "sanctification," in its verb form, simply means "to make holy." If we were to talk about the *what* of holiness—what it looks like—we could come up with a list of perceivable qualities; for example, a holy person might display purity, power, character, and love, among other characteristics of Christlikeness. But we must also ask the question of the *how* of holiness. How do we develop these qualities? How are we made holy? How are we sanctified?

In the epigraph texts from 1 Thessalonians, it is clear that God both wills holiness for us and that God is the one who does the sanctifying—the "holifying." We are also told that the sanctification God does is thorough, or comprehensive; it touches every part of our being. Yet we are still left with questions about how being sanctified—being made holy—plays itself out in a Christian's life. It would do us well to stop using the word "sanctification" because it is a noun. When we use a noun, it can become a static thing that we possess. Grammatically and theologically, we are always *being sanctified.* It is a verb, through and through. And it is God who sanctifies in an ongoing way.

There are actually four types of sanctification in Wesleyan-Holiness theology: initial, progressive, entire, and final. Sometimes we collapse the meaning of "sanctification" into a type of shorthand for what we call *entire* sanctification. It is an easy mistake to make. Long adherents of any tradition always grow accustomed to using language as a shortcut. To be theologically technical, the process of becoming holy—or *being sanctified*—begins when a person is born again, and the process of sanctification continues throughout one's life. The word "sanctification" should never be limited to one instantaneous event. Holiness is a *way of being,* not a one-time crisis experience or occurrence. Entire sanctification is one of the important means that brings this way of being about in a Christian's life—but it is not the only means.

At birth, each person is offered prevenient grace, which Wesleyans believe will draw them toward the choice of whether to be in a saving relationship with God. If the person cooperates with this grace and chooses to enter a relationship with God, saving grace is given, and a conversion moment results through faith in Jesus Christ. At this same point, the process of being sanctified begins with what is called "initial sanctification" (technically, *being initially sanctified)*: God gives us righteousness—or holiness—because of Christ; indeed, Christ is our righteousness and forgives our sin. Further, God begins to impart that righteousness in such a way that the person begins to actually be made holy (a present-tense verb). In other words, God does not merely perceive us *through* Christ's righteousness, as if we are clothed with a white robe that hides our sinful nature. God is intent on making us *actually* righteous or holy, which results in holy character and actions as we grow.

Being forgiven and being sanctified deals with our sin; even deeper, it begins to deal with our sinful nature. We receive new birth at conversion, when God begins to bring about this sanctifying process of spiritual development. Then "progressive sanctification" (or *being progressively sanctified*) follows. This part of the process can also be called gradual sanctification, growth in grace, or even spiritual formation. As growth occurs, the person will later be drawn to a place where an even fuller relational commitment to God is possible, marking the moment of "entire sanctification" (or *being entirely sanctified*).

After this deeper work of grace takes place, progressive sanctification again follows. Growth continues, through sustained entire devotion, until the person dies, at which point they then experience "final sanctification" (or *being finally sanctified*)—also known as "glorification."

It is certainly worth our time to go over the first three of these types of *being* sanctified in more detail. Remember, whenever you see the noun form of the word "sanctify," train your brain to think of it in its verb form instead.

Initial Sanctification as New Birth

Initial sanctification is one of the aspects of personal salvation. When we accept Christ through faith, many different things happen simultaneously. We are justified, adopted, redeemed, regenerated, and reconciled to God. When we are saved, all these transforming features happen to us—they have different meanings that help us understand the depth and breadth of our conversion.

To be *justified* is another way of saying we are forgiven—that God has taken the guilt of our past sins away from us. Our sins are thrown into the sea of forgetfulness (see Micah 7:19), as far as the east is from the west (see Psalm 103:12), and our sins are no longer counted against us because of what Christ did on the cross, which ultimately shows us God's unfathomable love for us.

To be *adopted* means we have become God's children in a new way. We are Christ's siblings. As co-heirs with Christ, we receive all the benefits of those who are part of God's family.

To understand how we are *redeemed*, we remember the exodus—God's people set free from slavery to move into a new future. In the same way, we are set free from our sins and from what may bind us in chains, and we are set on a new course.

To be *regenerated* means to be born anew; we experience *new birth* and are restored to such a degree that we are new creations; the old is gone. The concept of new birth was especially important to Wesley, who equated it with the beginning of being sanctified, pushing Wesley further from his Calvinist counterparts, who emphasized justification as primary.

The heart of all this is that we are *reconciled* to God. We enter into a new divine-human relationship, when our sin and brokenness need not separate us any longer from what God has created us to be. To be all God created us to be means to be renewed in the image of God—another way to describe sanctification.

All of this transformation *initiates* at the beginning of our relationship with God, where God begins the process of making us holy and spiritually whole. This is initial sanctification.

Progressive Sanctification as Growing in Grace

In his mature thought, Wesley strongly admonished Methodists—particularly the ministers and teachers—to emphasize both entire sanctification and progressive sanctification and not to neglect either. When we talk about growing in grace, we are really talking about progressive sanctification. In recent years, there has been a revived interest in Wesley's understanding of the day-by-day walk in the Christian journey. This resurgence has come both from

Grammatically and theologically,
we are always *being sanctified*.

a renewed emphasis on the means of grace in the Wesleyan tradition, as well as a great interest in the topic of spiritual formation more generally. It is important to note here that grace should not be seen as an abstract concept. Grace can be equated with the activity of the Holy Spirit; as such, we should see the means of grace as the means to experience and be nurtured by the very presence of God. This presence spiritually forms us, *transforming* us into the holy likeness of Christ. (See chapter 7 for more about the means of grace.)

As human beings, our spirituality is not detached from our physical, emotional, and cognitive development. Spiritual maturity is related to a person's maturity on the whole. Research has been done on faith development as it relates to different stages in life's journey from sociological and psychological dynamics. It is beyond our scope to outline this topic fully, but such research is crucial as a means of keeping us from expecting too much too soon spiritually, and not realizing human development is a major factor. For example, it is now understood that the brain does not fully develop until we are in our twenties, which means our moral and cognitive development are delayed beyond what we have historically assumed. As such, things like impulse control and delayed gratification are more difficult for children and teenagers. We should also factor in the reality that trauma affects development significantly, and trauma affects spiritual growth negatively, especially if the trauma is a result of religious or spiritual abuse. What all this means is that we should ask a question about what being sanctified at the age of fourteen *means*, as compared to the age of thirty, for example, and take into account how trauma can significantly derail a person's ability to trust, even God.

Entire Sanctification as Entire Devotion

Entire sanctification is when God draws us to the question: *Will you love and serve me, no matter what?* Or, *Will you give me all that you have and all that you are so you might experience my grace and my presence in such a way that you can reflect my image as Christlikeness more lovingly and consistently?* As always, God does more than ask us a question; God also provides what we need to respond.

Full consecration is not a work we do on our own. Wesleyan-Holiness theology is thoroughly optimistic about what the grace of God can do in the Christian life, especially when we are as open to that grace as we can be in a given moment through entire devotion. Although we take the power of sin seriously, Wesleyans ultimately believe that the power of grace is stronger than the power of sin. In a sense, this is what separates Wesleyanism from other traditions. Persons can anticipate more in life here and now (as opposed to only in heaven)—real transformation, significant growth in Christlikeness, and power over habitual sin.

As Paul says in Romans, "where sin increased, grace increased all the more" (5:20). This theology is perhaps best displayed in Romans 5–8. The latter part of Romans 7 gives insight into the human struggle against sin. Paul describes a person whose master is sin. Whatever that person intends to do in striving for the good, they are unable to do it on their own. Likewise, whatever evil they wish to avoid, those are the things that end up being carried out. Paul gives a vivid picture of the internal struggle of such an individual, whom Paul says is under the law and not under grace.

Interpretations of this passage are varied, but it is clear for Wesleyans that Paul is not describing his current situation, even though he uses the historical present as his verb tense. To reach this conclusion, one only needs to read what follows in Romans 8. What Paul talks about in Romans 7 is *not* to be descriptive of a saved, redeemed, or sanctified Christian's experience. There is more victory in life than perpetual slavery to sin.

It is perhaps hard for us today to experientially relate to Paul's metaphor of mastery. While we might be able to intellectually understand, it fails to communicate as effectively as it once did. Perhaps a more relevant metaphor would be related to addiction. Someone who is addicted to something is consumed by the drive to satisfy the desire or craving. It is almost as if they *cannot* do otherwise. Trying to ignore the addiction seems impossible. The person begins to be shaped by the addiction as it moves into the central place in heart and mind, which in turn affects and drives everything else the person does. An overwhelming feeling of being completely out of control of their own choices becomes dominant.

In Paul's portrayal of this type of situation, sinful desire ("the flesh") is almost personified as the entity that wars against the good, and against the good purposes to which we are all called, and against the purposes for which we were created. Finally, Paul throws up his hands and cries: "Who will rescue me from this body that is subject to death?" (7:24). Clearly, Paul's question is not the end of the story, yet some traditions do use this passage in Romans 7 to describe the Christian life until the person is rescued from life on earth and taken to heaven. Wesleyan-Holiness theology strongly affirms that the rescue for which Paul cries is possible here on earth through the grace of God and, more specifically, through the indwelling presence of the Holy Spirit. For this, Paul also cries, "Thanks be to God!" (v. 25).

In Romans 8 he continues, "Because through Christ Jesus the law of the Spirit who gives life has set you free from the law of sin and death. For what the law was powerless to do because it was weakened by the flesh, *God did* by sending his own Son . . . in order that the righteous requirement of the law might be fully met in us, who do not live according to the flesh but according to the Spirit" (vv. 2–3a, 4, emphasis added). These verses offer us three important aspects of holiness theology.

First, we are powerless to free ourselves from the addictive life of sin. Two words in this passage should stand out to us—indeed, shout to us the crucial truth of the gospel: the two words "God did." God took the initiative to free us from a life of bondage. We cannot save ourselves, we cannot sanctify ourselves, and we cannot break the power of sin by our own strength, no matter how pure our intentions or how hard we try. God must intervene.

Second, because of God's power, "the righteous requirement of the law" can be fully met in us—not met a bit, or partially, but *fully* met in us. Such a feat would be impossible in our own strength, but it is possible because of what God has accomplished in Christ. Is this language a call back to a type of perfectionism or legalism? If it were, Paul would contradict the entire theme of Romans, which is that our righteousness comes from grace through faith— through Christ's own holiness. But it is a righteousness that goes further than Christ's imputation. Imputation indicates that God might perceive us as holy, but we are still sinful in nature and action if one looks too closely beneath the holiness Jesus covers us with. The righteousness, or holiness, to which Paul calls us is imparted to us through grace. We are truly transformed in our inner being, and in response to this transformation, holiness becomes not only possible but *real.* Jesus's holiness makes us actually clean through the activity of the Holy Spirit. And, as Paul will state later in Romans 13:10, the law of love enables us to live the holiness we proclaim. Does that mean that we never sin? We never lose our ability (free will) to sin. But in the Wesleyan-Holiness tradition, sin isn't the last word! Also of note— all metaphors break down eventually, and the metaphor of addiction breaks down at this point. While cultural and scientific conversations about addiction seem to indicate that one can never truly be free of addiction, the Wesleyan-Holiness tradition holds that, in Christ, the addiction

Nothing will ever take away our *ability* to sin. But the sanctified, Spirit-filled life does effectively deal with our *propensity* to sin.

to sin breaks so significantly that the label of "sinner" no longer applies.

Third, Paul clearly reminds us that grace is not a static "thing" given at particular moments in our Christian life. Rather grace operates in a dynamic, living, growing, daily participation in the life of God. To express this truth, Paul calls us to "live . . . according to the Spirit" (8:4). We are called to life in the Spirit: "For those who are led by the Spirit of God are the children of God" (v. 14). Beautiful metaphors that Wesley accepted from the early church period inform us that our whole life is joined together with the love of the Trinity: we are *taken up into God* and are therefore transformed by the love of the three Persons as we participate in the divine dance. If sin is the separation of God's human creatures from the Eternal Source of life, then salvation lies in our inclusion into the community of God's eternal life. The mystery is this: Jesus takes us into an intimate relationship with God, through the Spirit; those who abide in love abide in God, and God abides in them. Or, as Ephesians says, "you may be filled to the measure of all the fullness of God" (3:19).

In sum, the Christian life—sustained by grace and the indwelling of the Holy Spirit—is a life of power, even power over sin. Wesley himself was tired of the question of whether that power implied absolute sinlessness. He believed that the question missed the point, which is that the sanctified life is no longer in bondage to the power of sin. Wesley faced a controversy in one of his societies when the leaders said directly that sanctification leaves a person *incapable* of sin. He countered this assertion strongly and took measures to remove the leadership and set the society straight theologically. Nothing will ever take away our *ability* to sin. But the sanctified, Spirit-filled life does effectively deal with our *propensity* to sin. The power of God, and the power of divine love, are greater than the power of sin in the here and now.

Although progressive sanctification is also, of course, subsequent to regeneration, entire sanctification most often happens at a point of decision. This decision has an effect on sin. The difference between Wesleyan-Holiness theology and the Reformed tradition is that we believe the power of sin can be effectively dealt with (broken, cleansed) so that we might live victoriously in this life. Consecrating everything—ourselves, our possessions, our family and friends, our pasts, and our futures—to God and committing our whole being to God's service is the first requisite of the entirely sanctified life.

When the power of sin is affected by grace, we are filled with a new power through the Holy Spirit to reflect God's deepest desires for us. Our intentions are purified, and our capacity to love grows into a true ability to love. Our inner disposition to sin is taken away, but immediately the abiding presence of the Spirit dwells within us in deeper and more pervasive ways than ever before—not because God has been stingy with grace before this moment but because we are as open as we have ever been to the presence of God, which sanctifies. Wesley was referring to this reality when he said that love excludes sin; love is poured into our hearts to such a degree that there is no more room for sin to rule.

John Wesley took Martin Luther's doctrine of *sola fide* ("faith alone") and applied it to the second work of grace. Just as we can do nothing to deserve salvation, we also can do nothing to deserve sanctification. We can *cooperate* with the grace of God, but we cannot *earn* the grace of God. One of Wesley's most important doctrines is the witness of the Spirit, also known as the doctrine of assurance. "The Spirit himself testifies with our spirit that we are God's children" (Romans 8:16). Wesley applied this thinking to the experience of entire sanctification: God will *assure* us that we have allowed God to do the deeper work and that sanctifying grace has filled us. (Of note: Wesley was aware later in his life that, because of non-spiritual factors [such as perhaps mental illness, in today's terms], it is conceivable for a person to be sanctified yet unable to experience this inner assurance. But he anticipated assurance for most Christians.)

Several metaphorical phrases can be used to describe entire sanctification. No one phrasing is necessarily better than another. Although certain periods of history have preferred particular wordings over others, none is normatively dominant. All language is metaphorical in a sense. New metaphors should arise for, and from, new generations, different cultures, and various geographic locations. It is also important that we allow persons to experience entire sanctification differently. We cannot put the experience in a box and limit the various ways the Holy Spirit works in individuals. Entire sanctification requires growth that must be intentionally nurtured. Entire sanctification is far from the end. We do not "arrive." The experience of entire sanctification enables us to grow without some of our previous encumbrances.

There is a key difference between a pure heart and Christian maturity. To have our heart purified gives us new potential, but it is still the maturing, growing process that realizes, more and more, this potential. It is absolutely key to acknowledge and proclaim that this growth is growth in Christlike character. We must always consider the goal of the Christian journey to be becoming more and more like Christ in his unconditional love toward all. This goal is definitive and normative of the sanctified life, with Christ's love at the forefront of our understanding of the character of God. After the experience of consecration and entire sanctification, we return to progressive sanctification until the end of our lives. We are not "done" when we devote ourselves to God entirely. That devotion must be lived out daily, which leads to even more growth in love and virtue. At times, when new circumstances arrive in our lives, our consecration may need to be ratified again and again. These are not new entire sanctification experiences but are connected to our progressive growth toward the full restoration of the image of God in us when we see God fully in the life to come.

Outward Signs of Inward Grace

It is traditional to talk about the outward signs of inward grace in terms of participating in the sacraments. We will indeed turn there momentarily, but we can also speak of it more generally. What are the outward signs, or evidence, of our initial, progressive, and entire sanctification?

The phrase "outward sign of inward grace" is used often in reference to baptism. Yes, our baptism is an outward sign of grace. If we are baptized as an infant, our baptism is a sign of prevenient grace—the grace that goes before. Prevenient grace leads us, as we grow and develop, to one day repent of our sins against God and against others, and to know the saving grace of God. If we are not baptized as children, and come to a saving knowledge of Jesus Christ later, we are baptized in celebration and affirmation of the justifying and initially sanctifying grace of God at work in us. In either case, the grace is signified in the waters of baptism (though baptism is not the *cause* of that grace; faith is always the precursor of grace, not the water itself).

In times of trouble and temptation, we can cry out, as Martin Luther explained and exclaimed, "I am baptized." This cry reminds us, *I am a child of God*. We remember our baptism as a symbol of our adoption into the family of God and as a reminder of the presence of the Holy Spirit. Sin and Satan have no hold on us. For Luther, baptism signified outwardly the beginning of a long spiritual journey with Christ—but one that we do not take alone. "The longer we live we become gentler, more patient, meeker, and ever with-draw more and more from unbelief, avarice, hatred, envy, haughtiness." Thus, by the power of baptism the old human (a biblical metaphor for the sinful nature) "daily decreases until he finally perishes." Luther concludes, "Thus it appears what a great, excellent thing baptism is, which delivers us from the jaws of the devil and makes us God's own, sup-presses and takes away sin, and then daily strengthens the new [person]; and is and remains ever efficacious until we pass from this estate of misery to eternal glory."[1]

For those who come to be baptized as adults, especial-ly in places where Christianity does not dominate in the world, to be baptized is to publicly declare not only to one's family and church but also to one's society that a person has decided—no matter the cost, no matter the persecu-tion or public humiliation—to identify as a Christian. The sacrament of baptism comes after great deliberation. Some churches require that a family member also be baptized because, they feel, it is impossible to be a Christian alone. For many, baptism is the identifying point at which one be-comes a Christian. It has also signified from the beginning that we are initiated into the church. A company of God's people accompany us on the pilgrimage, and Christian life is a daily working out of our baptism in the context of the church community.

For those who are baptized as infants, it is similar. They are baptized because they are born in a Christian home. Their parents will raise them as Christians. Their village is Christian. What else would they be? Some expe-rience great perplexity when asked when they became a Christian. They have always been a Christian. A few might answer, "I was a Christian before I was born." Their infant

---

1. Luther, "Baptism," in *The Large Catechism*, https://www.creeds.net/luther-an/luther_large.htm.

baptism is an outward sign of the inward grace they have already received from the atonement of Christ.

In either case, whether baptized as infants or as adults, most evangelicals, including those in the Wesleyan tradition, affirm that baptism is not what saves us. Certainly, we may see in heaven some who were never baptized. But the practice of baptism should be normative for the church as the primary sign of initiation into the kingdom of God.

Outward Signs of Sanctifying Grace

What are the outward signs, or evidence, of our initial, progressive, and entire sanctification? Are there outward signs of this inward grace that flows from the atonement of Christ, through the moment-by-moment movement of the Holy Spirit, by which we are cleansed within and maturing in love?

Within the Anglican tradition (from which the Methodist Church and, subsequently, the Holiness Movement sprang), stemming from much earlier practices and theologies of the church, there was a second work of grace of sanctification called "confirmation," coming after the first work, signified by baptism. The effect of confirmation, said the great Catholic theologian Thomas Aquinas, "is that the Holy Spirit is imparted to give strength, just as he was given to the Apostles on the day of Pentecost. Thus, the Christian must boldly confess the name of Christ [in confirmation]."[2] Confirmation was to enable growth in maturity and perfection in love. In Anglican confirmation, believers affirm their full commitment to God on the basis of both knowledge and desire. Confirmation represents that, after baptism with water and the Holy Spirit, there comes a strengthening grace through the same Holy Spirit, who ev-

---

2. *The Catechetical Instructions of St. Thomas Aquinas* (1939; reprint, Manila: Sinag-Tala, n.d.), 146.

ery day brings wisdom, counsel, knowledge, and true god-
liness. Some in the Methodist Church have also returned to
this practice and ceremony, although John Wesley himself
never suggested that the sanctifying grace he preached
could or would be received through confirmation.[3] Some
in Holiness denominations have also called for a return to
confirmation as a sacramental practice.

Wesley was more optimistic that sanctifying grace
could and would be received during the time of holy Communion. The collective prayer, prayed at all Anglican Communion services, and now prayed at many Methodist and
Wesleyan-Holiness services, was a prayer for cleansing and
sanctifying grace: "Almighty God, unto whom all hearts be
open, all desires known, and from whom no secrets are hid:
Cleanse the thoughts of our hearts by the inspiration of thy
Holy Spirit, that we may perfectly love thee, and worthily
magnify thy holy Name; through Christ our Lord. Amen."[4]
For the Church of the Nazarene, Communion is "a means
of grace in which Christ is present by the Spirit."[5] Communion is a transforming sacrament where one can meet
Christ and receive, according to Wesley, prevenient, justifying, or sanctifying grace. Through the words of the ritual we
hear the good news and have the opportunity of praying for
and receiving sanctifying grace.

---

3. John Fletcher was clearer than John Wesley in seeing the theological connection between entire sanctification and confirmation as second works of grace.
See Laurence W. Wood, *Pentecost and Sanctification in the Writings of John Wesley
and Charles Wesley: With a Proposal for Today* (Lexington, KY: Emeth Press, 2018),
9–18, 249–59; see in the same volume Jeremy Taylor, "Discourse on Confirmation," 295–320.

4. The Church of England, "The Lord's Supper or Holy Communion: The
Order for the Administration of the Lord's Supper or Holy Communion," https://
www.churchofengland.org/prayer-and-worship/worship-texts-and-resources/
book-common-prayer/lords-supper-or-holy-communion#na.

5. Church of the Nazarene, "I. Sacraments: 700. Lord's Supper," *Manual:
2017–2021* (Kansas City, MO: Nazarene Publishing House, 2017), 260.

The nineteenth-century Holiness Movement, and the evangelical movement more broadly, introduced the use of the kneeling rail—or mourner's bench, later called the altar—as a place to come and make a spiritual decision after a sermon. The Holiness Movement stressed that, just as the outward mark of justifying grace was bowing at an altar of prayer, often during a revival service or camp meeting, the outward mark of sanctifying grace would be similar: moved by the Holy Spirit, surrounded by a community of like-minded believers, in a moment of utter consecration of oneself, one would invite into one's life a grace that would sanctify through and through. Being able to *identify* the moment of entire sanctification and testify to it—just as one could identify the moment of being born again—was considered to be the most important outward sign of inward sanctifying grace. Generations of Holiness evangelists encouraged those who believed they had been entirely sanctified to testify to it immediately. In doing so, they would seal the experience. More than that, testifying to sanctifying grace before one's family and community of faith meant others would then have certain expectations of one's behavior and lifestyle.

When we focus upon a particular juncture in time—like the moment of entire sanctification—*as our most significant* outward sign of inward grace, we are in danger of placing the circumstance of holiness above the content of holiness—making a person's testimony to a particular moment in time more important than how that person lived out the sanctified life from that point forward. For those who could so testify, what could we say if they were racist or acted unkindly toward their spouse or children, or their fellow believers, even after their testified experience of sanctification? In some cases, we became known as a judgmental, scolding, nagging people who concentrated our attention on external righteousness, rather than on the charity and grace that might allow us to distinguish between essentials and nonessentials. Sometimes we have failed to show care, respect, compassion, forgiveness, and redemptive love. Mildred Bangs Wynkoop said:

Perfectionism may manifest itself in *moralism*. *External conformity to law is of prior importance.* Every human act is regulated by law. The law becomes so complex and intricate that dress styles and colors for both men and women, recreational possibilities, and every minutia of personal and corporate life are carefully proscribed. Holiness is measured by this conformity. That a very unpleasant and harsh spirit may accompany this conformity is no argument against it. In fact, it is said, harshness is needed to maintain it and is finally considered to be a sign and assurance of perfection and sanctity. When human beings take over the task of the Holy Spirit in keeping one's neighbor pure, the job is too big and force supersedes persuasion, and becomes a virtue.[6]

The specific outward expectations of the community of faith indeed became important signs of inward sanctifying grace—to the point that a type of strict legalism began to show. There came to be expectations about giving up worldly vices—chiefly tobacco and alcohol consumption—and the list only lengthened through the years. Living by outward signs of behavior became paramount, to the point that Christ's judgment of the Pharisees—that the outside of the cup was clean while the inside was corrupt (Matthew 23:25)—could be rightly directed toward Holiness people.

One could identify a Christian under this model by what they did and did not do, where they went and did not go. Women in particular were watched closely. In some

6. Mildred Bangs Wynkoop, *A Theology of Love: The Dynamic of Wesleyanism*, 2nd ed. (Kansas City, MO: Beacon Hill Press of Kansas City, 2015), 282.

places and times, Christian women did not cut their hair or wear makeup or jewelry (some being so strict as to not even wear a wedding ring). Indeed, guidelines for Christian behavior, assessed by a broad community of faith, rather than by individuals alone, can be good—in fact, crucial. We need ethical guidelines and wisdom beyond ourselves. However, problems arise when outward rules of behavior are equated with sanctification, when legalism becomes synonymous with holiness. Pursuing holiness became reduced to evidence that Christians did not, for example, play billiards or go bowling (for those were places where people gambled). Yet these same people prohibited those with skin of a different color than theirs from entering their church sanctuaries. They did not practice justice and mercy. They were strict in outward behavior and prejudiced and unloving in their hearts.

After controversies on rules arose in the Church of the Nazarene in the 1950s, General Superintendent G. B. Williamson wrote in the *Herald of Holiness* (now *Holiness Today*), the denomination's magazine, so that all Nazarenes could see it, that although it was "the duty of the church to raise high standards of morality," to defend legalism was "to isolate the church and force upon it the loss of contact with the world it is designed to redeem." Legalism, he said, became "a deadly wound" that produced a "decadent, ingrown, pharisaical sect."[7] Indeed, like the Pharisees and teachers of the law, some equated holiness with strictness in keeping laws and in adding law upon law, prohibition upon prohibition, replacing the gospel of grace, and finally arriving at a moralism that looked nothing like Jesus.

Though the list of behavioral prohibitions sometimes seemed arbitrary, certainly not all aspects were. Why give

---

7. G.B. Williamson, "Enlarge the Outer Court," *Herald of Holiness* 46 (September 18, 1957): 1.

up alcohol, for instance? Not only Holiness people, but others as well had come to see the devastating effects of liquor upon families and societies. So much liquor was consumed among U.S. Americans in the pre-Civil War period that one historian called it the "alcoholic republic." Women beaten and abused by drunk husbands came running to rescue missions. Alcohol-addicted men and women could not keep their jobs. Children suffered. Some could drink socially, and it never became a problem; others could not. The devastation that resulted from alcohol called early Holiness groups to stand in solidarity with those it so negatively affected. It wasn't prudishness but genuine love for the abused and downtrodden that motivated this stance.

Let us go back to Wesley for a moment. What were his expectations as outward signs of inward, sanctifying grace? Since his evangelism predated altar calls, that was not the means by which a person came to pray for either new birth or entire sanctification; a specific date was not the focus. Second, early in his ministry Wesley had great doubts that a person could be entirely sanctified until shortly before death. But then, he reasoned, if entirely sanctified upon the deathbed, and the person recovered, would not the grace be retained? This consideration led him to believe, and subsequently preach, that entire sanctification could happen well before death (a belief his brother Charles opposed).

Additionally, if one believed that the Holy Spirit had wholly sanctified them, there would be, as with justification, evidence of the Holy Spirit bearing witness within. Wesley admonished, however, that one should wait before testifying to sanctifying grace until, perhaps, one might hear some kind of confirmation from an external source, such as, "Dear friend, I have seen a difference in you. You seem to be more patient than before, more loving, more generous, different in how you speak, different in how you react. What has brought the change?" Then Wesley allowed that the person might say something like, "I believe that the Holy Spirit of God sanctifies me." One would not say, "I *am* sanctified" but, "I am *being* sanctified" because progressive sanctification follows entire sanctification.

For Wesley, sanctification was evident when a person bore the *fruit* of the Spirit in their own life in an ongoing way. You would see it yourself. Your friends would see it. Your children would see it. Your spouse would see it. In fact, it was probably better than asking persons whether they had a moment when they were entirely sanctified, to ask their spouse, in the present moment! In sum, the outward signs of inward, sanctifying grace would be primarily the fruit of the Spirit (see Galatians 5:22–23), and especially Christlike love. Sanctifying grace is indeed an inward grace, but it is also demonstrable.

Wesley affirmed all of the fruit of the Spirit but especially lifted up what the King James Version calls "temperance" and what other, more modern versions translate as "self-control." It signified more than controlling oneself away from sin. Wesley's emphasis was upon simplicity of life. One lived simply, simply for the sake of others. Even if one had the money to live ostentatiously, grandly, luxuriously, one should not, for it would limit the ability to live generously and hospitably for the sake of others, said Wesley. One gave for the sake of the poor. If there was anyone more pessimistic, and harder on the rich and wealthy coming to Christ than John Wesley, it would be Jesus. An outward sign was visiting and befriending the poor, and others unlike oneself. The privilege of friendship with those who were marginalized transformed perspectives on how one governed one's own life.

These outward signs of inner sanctifying grace enact the principles of the kingdom of God as Christ preached it. In this sense, the kingdom is near. When people truly live into the Sermon on the Mount, display the love of God as perfected by Christ, and produce the fruit of the Spirit, the kingdom of heaven becomes the kingdom on earth. We anticipate the day when all will be made new.

Final Sanctification and Glorification

Final sanctification comes with the restoration of all creation or when we die, whichever comes first. Final sanctification has also traditionally been called "glorification" because we will actually be in the very presence of the Trinity. In one sense, our sanctification will be complete. In another sense, our purpose—which is to reflect the image of God and glorify God—will never end. Our purpose to love one another as God loves us will never end. In what sense will that love grow in us, even after the culmination of time as we know it? We can only speculate. What we do know is that God calls us to fulfill our purpose here and now (more on that in chapter 8).

SEVEN

The Path to Virtue

Therefore, as God's chosen people, holy and dearly loved, clothe yourselves with compassion, kindness, humility, gentleness and patience. Bear with each other and forgive one another if any of you has a grievance against someone. Forgive as the Lord forgave you. And over all these virtues put on love, which binds them all together in perfect unity.

Let the peace of Christ rule in your hearts, since as members of one body you were called to peace. And be thankful. Let the message of Christ dwell among you richly as you teach and admonish one another with all wisdom through psalms, hymns, and songs from the Spirit, singing to God with gratitude in your hearts. And whatever you do, whether in word or deed, do it all in the name of the Lord Jesus, giving thanks to God the Father through him.

—Colossians 3:12–17

We continue the discussion from the last chapter on the fruit of the Spirit with an exploration here of character and virtue. Grace changes our character if we receive it and co-operate with it. The result will be actions that parallel that changed character. Wesley wrote an interesting work called "The Character of a Methodist," where he explores what holiness looks like when it is lived out. It clearly shows us that our actions spring out of what God has done within us at important moments and over time as we mature. The character of a Methodist according to Wesley:

1. Loves God with all the heart, soul, mind, and strength
2. Gives thanks in everything
3. Has a heart lifted to God at all times
4. Loves every person as his or her own soul
5. Is pure in heart
6. Evidences that God reigns in the heart alone, without rival or idols
7. Keeps all the commandments
8. Does all to the glory of God
9. Adorns the doctrine of God in all things[1]

These characteristics represent a pretty high standard of living, and the Wesleyan-Holiness tradition believes it is possible to live with such character. Another word for character is "integrity," which we can think of in the sense of being *integrated*—it means our insides consistently match our outsides, so to speak. We can act like holy people because we have become people of integrity by the grace of God. "Virtue" is another word that can be used in place of high character or integrity.

Prior to Wesley's century (the 1700s), Anglicanism was greatly influenced by the intellectualist model of ethical theory. This theory suggests that reason—the mind—should be the superior human attribute in all decisions about morality, with the passions—emotions—as something to fight. Here we would find Plato's idea that to *know* the good is to *do* the good. This theory says that all we need in order to be ethical is to decide (reason) to do the right thing.

For example, say I decide to start exercising so I can live longer for the people who depend on me. I read books

---

1. John Wesley, "The Character of a Methodist" in *The Works of John Wesley*, Thomas Jackson, ed. (Grand Rapids: Baker, 1979), 8:340–351.

that show me how incredibly beneficial exercise can be for one's health. I am convinced. I talk to friends who have started exercise programs in the past. They testify how much better they feel and how good their blood work is whenever they see their doctor. One even had an unhealthy heart until he became serious about diet and exercise. I absolutely believe what I am being told. So I set an exercise schedule for myself and set a date to get up at six a.m. to walk three miles before work. Then, on that date, I turned off my alarm. I did the same thing the next day. I knew the data. I believed the testimony of others. I even *decided* to do it. In my mind, I knew the good I ought to have done. But I *didn't* do it. If Plato is right—that if I know the good, then I will do the good—then what went wrong? Paul knew real life doesn't seem to work that way. If it did, then acting wrongly, or sinning, would be a matter of ignorance only, not an act of willful intention. Ethical action flows from right reason, say the intellectualists.

As empiricism gained popularity during the Enlightenment, so did the idea that emotions (or "affections") are also important to any internal motivation to act ethically. Wesley approved of this change away from the intellectualist model and toward valuing affections so much that he developed a moral psychology that accounted for the vital role of affections.[2] His list of elements that affected and determined ethical behavior included, alongside the mind: the will, understanding, liberty, conscience, and certainly the heart as the central force beneath moral living. A crucial distinction from an intellectualist model is what Wesley meant by "the will." He believed the will was influenced not only by reason but also by the affections, and perhaps *only* by the affections. In other words, willing was more a

---

2. Randy Maddox, "Holiness of Heart and Life: Lessons from North American Methodism," *Asbury Theological Journal* 51 (1996): 152–53.

function of affections that reside in the heart than an act of "rational self-determination."[3]

What did Wesley mean by the word "affections"? Affections are habituated emotions that lead to motivating inclinations over time, rather than just momentary emotions. We can intentionally habituate affections and inclinations through practice and eventually act out what we are thus inclined to do. Theologically speaking, the affections are influenced by outside causes—most particularly grace. Wesley did not stop there. He believed that the affections and inclinations are habituated into *enduring dispositions*, which he called "tempers." We act out of these habituated and grace-filled dispositions. In other words, we act out of right-hearted tempers—a heart purified and empowered by God that has been transformed over time. The best example of a temper for Wesley is love for God and neighbor. When love fills the heart, this holy temper becomes holy action—at times expressing itself in the negation of one thing for the sake of another but most often as positive, loving action. We act lovingly because our hearts have been changed, inclined, and disposed to love.

For example, I play the trumpet. I first learned when I was eight years old. I was horrible at first, of course, and sounded like a dying elephant. With practice, I improved so much that I was first chair in the high school band. What did that practice do, exactly? Like most wind instruments, each note has a different fingering on the trumpet. At first, I would look at an A on a score of music and have to remind myself to push the two first valves at the same time. But the more I practiced, the more such details became part of my muscle memory. It wasn't long before I could play a piece of music without thinking about the fingering at all. With practice, I could also play harder and harder pieces. We

---

3. Maddox, "Holiness of Heart and Life," 153.

might even say that all that practice made me "free" to play the trumpet. It would be like second nature. I no longer just played the trumpet—I *was* a trumpeter. But if someone were to hand me a clarinet, I would not be able to play it; I am not free to play it. I might be able to blow into it, but I am certainly not a clarinetist.

Correspondingly, character operates the same way. Aided by grace, if I practice kindness over and over again, one might say that I am a kind person. Kind behavior *becomes* the virtue of kindness that has become part of who I am. We might say that I am now free to be kind in every new situation because it has become second nature to me. This acknowledgment does not mean I *will* always be kind since I am always free to act against what I have habitually (and by grace) become. But I am now *inclined* toward kindness. I am freer to do the kind act instead of the unkind act. I now have the disposition to be kind.

Wesley believed that the affections are *habituated into enduring dispositions*—the "tempers." Tempers reside in the heart; right tempers reside in the heart that has been made right; a right heart produces right action. But where in this is the grace of God?

In order to define further the meaning of inward and outward holiness, I will offer a description of what it means to be wholehearted, or full-hearted. Very often we have wrongly emphasized what I will call "empty-heartedness." Mildred Bangs Wynkoop has a rather simple idea that has profound and wide-reaching implications. The opposite of sin is not sinlessness. You cannot understand the nature of something by only referencing a vacuum, a black hole, an absence of something else. Yet holiness, as the opposite of sin, very often has been defined as sinlessness. The imperative goal was to rid one's life of sins of commission, which can lead to errant theology that implies that sinlessness is the goal of the Christian life. It is not!

Too often, we have been trained to be acutely aware of the activity of the devil around us, rather than the activity of the Holy Spirit.

Say you want to run a marathon and begin to train. You want to build stamina and improve the time it takes to finish. Your goals are endurance and speed. But there is a problem. Each time before you run, you eat five Big Macs. Your endurance and your speed certainly do not improve. Next, you determine that you will *not* eat the five Big Macs before you train. You say to yourself, "Thou shalt not eat five Big Macs." You start evangelizing about this basic principle to others. You gather followers. You now have a club that goes out and shares the message, one on one and through social media. It has become your mantra, your passion, and your purpose. Your and your club's entire focus becomes what you *do not eat*, and you eventually stop running at all, forgetting in your focused determination that the original goal was to run a marathon. You are content in what you do not do, and you sit sedentarily.

At times in our history, we have forgotten the true goal of the sanctified life when we have only focused on the "thou shalt nots." It is true that there are things we will not do, or will stop doing, when our hearts are being sanctified, but those are not our end goal. Jesus tells a small but powerful parable in Luke 11: "When an impure spirit comes out of a person, it goes through arid places seeking rest and does not find it. Then it says, 'I will return to the house I left.' When it arrives, it finds the house swept clean and put in order. Then it goes and takes seven other spirits more wicked than itself, and they go in and live there. And the final condition of that person is worse than the first" (vv. 24–26). If a house is swept clean, without something to replace the evil that once resided there, it remains vulnerable. Holiness is not just the *absence* of sin but the *presence* of love. A right heart, then, is a full heart—a heart full of love, brought by the *indwelling presence of the Holy Spirit*. The full heart acts lovingly.

The sanctified heart is full of love; the heart is so full of the love of God that sin is pushed out. That love takes up the full capacity of heart so that sin can no longer reign and, eventually, no longer remain. Out of a heart of love (or character of love), love becomes second nature to us as we practice it. It becomes our disposition, or temper. Out of a loving disposition, we act lovingly. The love of Christ at the center of our hearts keeps the holy in holiness. Only with love at the center of our hearts are we ever enabled to reflect the holy God and be holy as God is holy. This Christlike, cruciform love keeps our beliefs from becoming calcified and dead.

The Means of Grace

For Wesley, attending to the means of grace is the way our hearts become full to overflowing, reflecting virtue and true Christlike character. The more we participate in the means of grace, the more we *want* to participate in the means of grace, thereby drawing closer to God. Too often, persons remain only in a duty phase, and view the means of grace as regimented disciplines undertaken to prove ourselves loyal to God. Wesley takes us beyond sheer obedience for obedience's sake, beyond any type of works righteousness; Wesley emphasizes that participating in the means of grace is the precise way we grow and are transformed.

I like to use the analogy of a funnel. God has all the grace we need, and the funnel is the channel by which God's grace reaches us. Participating in the means of grace keeps that funnel open. Through the means of grace, we are given progressively sanctifying grace, which changes our affections, tempers, dispositions, and inclinations in that God's transforming grace reaches us through the means God has ordained. We become more fully who we are created to be in Christ by attending to the means of grace.

It is unfortunate that the words "spiritual disciplines" are sometimes substituted for "means of grace." The means of grace transcend discipline. Spiritual disciplines have been repeatedly explained using athletics as an analogy. Just as we must train our bodies through discipline in order to be successful in sports, we also must train ourselves spiritually in order to be successful as Christians. Paul himself uses the athlete as an example of perseverance (see 1 Corinthians 9:24–27). If we are not careful, we might begin to think we keep ourselves spiritually fit the same way we keep ourselves physically fit. God then becomes just a coach to give us pointers here and there. The analogy breaks down when we need to talk about the coach being *inside* the athlete, giving the athlete their strength. The means of grace avoid this analogical breakdown. Participating in the means of grace serves to remind us that all we do, all we are, and all we become is only possible through the grace of God within us through the presence of the Holy Spirit. Yes, sometimes such participation looks like discipline. But our discipline alone does not create and maintain Christlike character. Duty and discipline can focus our attention on our own efforts and away from the gracious activity of God in all facets of our lives.

There are three categories into which Wesley has placed certain activities under the means of grace. There are the general, the prudential, and the instituted (or particular) means of grace. These designations are how Wesley categorized Christian activities that have deep spiritual benefit to those who participate in them.

General Means of Grace

The general means of grace include universal obedience and keeping the commandments, watching, denying ourselves, taking up our cross, and exercising the presence of God.

Universal obedience and keeping the commandments are key in maintaining and fostering a relationship with God. We must remind ourselves that we are not earning grace through works. Think again of the funnel. If we live in disobedience or continue to break the commandments of God, it is not as if God then *withholds* grace. Rather, we have blocked the channel through our own action. In this case, repentance is the means by which we open the funnel again, opening ourselves again to receive the grace we need. If the offense is direct disobedience, we need the forgiving grace of God. Repentance is the way we synergistically cooperate with God because repentance always means we change how we do things—there is further work beyond *feeling* sorry. Obedience and keeping the commandments keeps the channel open between us and the God of mercy and compassion.

Watching is the intentional act of seeking God. The word "watching" itself implies we are *looking* for God's activity in the world. We are to have our eyes fixed on what is unseen to a greater degree than on what is seen (See 2 Corinthians 4:18). It is easy to forget this activity of watching, and to go through our day without purposefully looking for the hand of God in our lives, in the lives of those around us, and in the world. In light of our strong belief in God's prevenient grace, we should expectantly hope to see such work. Too often, we have been trained to be acutely aware of the activity of the devil around us, rather than the activity of the Holy Spirit. Watching is a means of grace that should be nurtured and deepened. This intentional attitude keeps us attuned and the channel of God's grace open.

By denying ourselves, Wesley believed we can draw closer to God when distractions are willingly set aside. In this context, self-denial is a means of grace because it keeps the channel open. This type of self-denial has a rich history, particularly in the writings of those in the early church.

The point was for them to find themselves detached from worldly concerns, even legitimate concerns, in order to be better able to pursue God. This practice is just as needed today as it was then, if not more. In a culture saturated with entertainment and consumerism, the ideas of simplicity, silence, and purposeful detachment are certainly countercultural. It has been said that persons who live in such a culture are attempting to numb themselves from their own generalized anxiety. If nothing else, self-denial can reveal to us how dependent we are on activities that keep us numbly occupied. The simple exercise of silence can show us exactly how much we have come to need noise. Self-denial in many forms can serve to refocus our attention and renew our entire devotion to and dependence on God.

By taking up our cross, Wesley believed we could also draw closer to God and God's purposes—first by enduring hardship and suffering for the sake of others, and second by doing things that go against our natural inclinations. This second meaning is the foil to self-denial. By feeding the poor, visiting those in prison, or taking care of widows and orphans (see Matthew 25:34–36 and James 1:27), our attention is drawn to what really matters. These actions are a means of grace in that we not only help others, but we ourselves also benefit from a proper perspective of what it means to be a disciple of Christ.

Exercising the presence of God is the practice of being conscious of God throughout the day, which is related to but different from watching. When watching, we are looking for the activity of the Holy Spirit around us. When practicing the presence of God, we are directly communing with God in all we do. This idea was made popular by a monk named Brother Lawrence. He attempted to be aware of God's presence in every minute of every day. That did not mean he only sat and prayed all day but that he took God with him, so to speak, into all his daily activities.

From working in the garden to washing the dishes, he was aware that God was with him always. Again, in light of all the distractions we face, exercising the presence of God is a difficult, but it is important to attempt. We may not practice God's presence perfectly, but any effort is better than no effort. If we affirm that the presence of God in our lives defines spirituality and aids Christian growth, then *practicing* that God is with us is just as important as *trusting* that God is with us. Many who have attempted such practice testify to the fact that it changed their hearts and lives.

Prudential Means of Grace

The prudential means of grace developed over time and have been recognized as prudent—or wise—actions in the life of growth in grace. Most involve other persons, rather than being strictly private acts of devotion.

The prudential means of grace include band and class meetings (or what many today call small groups) where accountability is stressed. Fellowship with other believers in a variety of contexts was crucial for Wesley, and should be for us today. Only when we engage in genuine and meaningful relationships do we grow toward our full potential. Love is never an abstract concept. Wesley was aware that not only do we need to love others, but we also need to receive the love of other Christians to encourage and support us. Wesley believed that prayer meetings are a means of grace that bring the body of Christ into purposeful prayer; such communal prayer differs from our own solitary prayers. Prayer meetings are an expression of agreeing together for God's will to be done, which the New Testament says is particularly efficacious (see Matthew 18:19–20).

We also find this communal aspect in Wesley's covenant and watch night services, which stress the need to reaffirm our commitments to be entirely devoted to God in the context of the church. Wesley's covenant service became extremely important for the Methodist people. It was a liturgy they recited in a deeply moving service that very much shows the warm-heartedness of the Methodist tradition. Traditionally, watch night services occur on New Year's Eve, when people gather to pledge another year of devotion and service to God.

Love feasts were also a time of communal renewal in Wesley's Methodism. Interestingly, these became controversial. Wesley intended these feasts to be a type of testimony service for the purpose of building up leaders and mature Christians. A person had to be in good standing and worthy to receive a ticket in order to attend. There was some protest as to why anyone should be excluded from these meetings, but Wesley maintained that mature Christians and leaders sometimes needed an opportunity to build one another up. Wesley was insightful on this point. Often leaders in the church spend the majority of their time taking care of the needs of the rest of the congregation (or societies, in Wesley's day). There do need to be intentional opportunities for leaders to be fed and nourished.

Another means of grace for Wesley was doing all the good one can and doing no harm. Wesley is famous for saying the following: *Do all the good you can, by all the means you can, in all the ways you can, in all the places you can, at all the times you can, to all the people you can, as long as ever you can.* Wesley is often quoted for the wisdom of these words, but he didn't intend them to be proverbial only; acting for the good is also personally transformative.

Wesley mentioned visiting the sick and poor specifically. Any legitimate theology of pastoral care will agree that this act is central. But how is it a means of grace? In a sense, visiting the sick and impoverished reminds us of our own frailty, and at times our own mortality; visiting the sick and the poor necessarily turns our minds and hearts toward the eternal. Sometimes the sick evidence God's grace in deep ways that can only affect our own sense of God's presence and sustaining power. Visiting the sick and the poor can also make us agents of God's love and mercy. Any time we are a conduit of God's love to others, we can experience that divine love in our own hearts.

Finally, Wesley found it so important to read devotional classics and edifying literature that he took great care to provide his people with significant Christian writing from throughout the centuries of Christianity because he believed God would grace those who pondered the wisdom of old. The grand, multivolume *Christian Library* was one of Wesley's greatest contributions to Methodist clergy education and to the spiritual nurture of laity. Although the whole collection is no longer published, individual works are still available. Books written by contemporary writers can certainly be inspiring, but like Wesley, we should be intentional to also read works that have stood the test of time.

Instituted or Particular Means of Grace

The "instituted" or "particular" means of grace refer to those means that Christ directly asks his disciples to do or models for them. Prayer and searching Scripture are foundational to all spiritual formation and transformation. It has been said that prayer is to the spiritual life as breathing is to the physical body. Without it, we do not survive. Wesley believed private prayer is only one form of prayer as a means of grace. He also stressed the importance of public and family prayer.

Another fundamental means of grace is "searching the Scriptures." The word "searching" implies a meditative reading where the Holy Spirit inspires our hearts. This approach is different from the study of Scripture for the purpose of doctrinal truth, although such study is also important. If prayer is our breath, Scripture is our food. Too often people read their Bibles out of a sense of duty. But using the analogy here, eating food is not a duty we perform. We need food in order to survive and thrive. From it we gain neces-

If we affirm that the presence of God in our lives defines spirituality and aids Christian growth, then *practicing* that God is with us is just as important as *trusting* that God is with us.

sary nutrients and the energy we need to do anything. Our bodies let us know when we need to eat. If we do not eat, we become weak and eventually start feeling the sensation of deep hunger that can lead to starvation. Interestingly, there comes a point in the starvation process when a person no longer feels hungry. In a similar way, we can neglect the spiritual food we need to the point of no longer feeling spiritually hungry. Perhaps like the physical body, then we are on the verge of spiritual death. If we read our Bibles because we are supposed to or as an act of sheer obedience, we misunderstand "searching the Scriptures" and miss its purpose as a key means of grace.

Wesley names fasting as an instituted means of grace, not just under the prudential category of general self-denial. Wesley practiced fasting food often, at least weekly. (Besides the spiritual benefit of drawing closer to God, some have seen this as perhaps contributing to his unusually long life.) The practice of fasting for its own sake seems to be waning in emphasis in the church today. Fasting a meal and giving the money for that meal to the needy is more common now than fasting for the sake of seeking earnestly the heart and will of God, or as an expression of penitence or spiritual desire. Regardless of how we fast—to help the needy or as a sign of particular devotion—it is a means of grace to us.

The next instituted means of grace is "Christian conference," or conversation. Wesley meant discussions between believers about our spirituality, not merely two or more Christians having a conversation about just anything. As Christians speak about God together, grace is poured out upon the participants. It is fascinating that we can attend church week after week and never say a word about our own personal spiritual journey. We can easily walk into Sunday school, catch up on each other's weeks, even open the Bible together and study it—all without saying a spiritually authentic thing about ourselves, or without inquiring about the spiritual lives of those we attend church with week after week. Christian conference, or conversation, like all the means of grace, is an intentional, purposeful, diligent act. It is an act of love as we share our faith and live "life together" in the very presence of the Holy Spirit.[4] The community of believers is intended to be a means of mutual support, encouragement, and strength. To experience this, we must foster spiritual vulnerability.

The final instituted means of grace we will discuss is that of the Lord's Supper (also known as holy Communion or Eucharist[5]). Rob Staples, in his book *Outward Sign and Inward Grace*, strongly reminds the Wesleyan-Holiness tradition of the appropriate understanding of the Christian sacraments. In this important work, he states that the Lord's Supper should be seen as a sacrament of sanctification. It will serve us well to quote one passage from Staples at length:

> Sanctification, which for Wesley has instantaneous aspects, is also a "progressive work, carried on in the soul by slow degrees, from the time of our first turning to God" (*Works* 6:74). One important means of furthering that sanctifying work is participation in the Lord's Supper. [William] Willimon is correct in saying: "The Lord's Supper is a 'sanctifying ordinance,' a sign of the continuity, necessity, and availability of God's enabling, communal, confirming, nurturing grace. Our characters are formed, sanctified, by such instruments of continual divine activity in our lives."[6] Persons brought up in the Wesleyan-Holiness

---

4. See Dietrich Bonhoeffer, *Life Together* (New York: Harper and Row Publishers, 1954).

5. Eucharist literally means "thanksgiving."

6. William Willimon, *The Service of God: Christian Work and Worship* (Nashville: Abingdon Press, 1983), 125. Quoted in Staples, *Outward Sign and Inward Grace*, 204.

churches have generally not been well instructed as to the potential of the Eucharist as a means for the promotion of holiness. For them, the very normality, regularity, and ritualistic nature of the sacrament militates against such an understanding. The invitation to the Lord's Supper is not particularly heard as a call to holiness. [And yet] "sanctification asserts that the Christian life ought not to be formed in a haphazard way. It takes constant, lifelong attention, habits, and care to employ this character. The normality, the constancy of the Eucharist is part of its power. This meal need not be special, nor exhilaratingly meaningful (though sometimes it is both). This is the normal food of Christians, the sustaining, nourishing stuff of our life"[7]. . . Whereas baptism is the sacrament of initiation and consequently is not repeated, the sacrament of sanctification is to be celebrated again and again from baptism until death.[8]

In his sermon "The Duty of Constant Communion," Wesley communicates strongly that the Eucharist should be celebrated constantly. He argued tenaciously against those who feared that frequency would diminish efficacy. Wesley could argue against this way of thinking because he saw Communion as an extremely significant means of grace. Should we pray less frequently because we fear it will lose its meaning? Should we read our Bibles less often, go to church less, minister to others less? Of course not. Then why fear that frequent celebration of Communion will make it less meaningful?

---

7. Willimon, *The Service of God*, 127. Quoted in Staples, *Outward Sign and Inward Grace*, 205.

8. Rob Staples, *Outward Sign and Inward Grace: The Place of Sacraments in Wesleyan Spirituality* (Kansas City, MO: Beacon Hill Press of Kansas City, 1991), 204–05.

The Eucharist in Wesley's eyes is a means by which the soul is peculiarly nourished. This does not mean Wesley believed in transubstantiation, or a literal changing of the elements.[9] The act, which involves memory as well as the direct activity of the Holy Spirit, is an immediate way (as in *immediacy*) of participating in the ongoing, transforming grace of God. As such, it should not be neglected. Yet, as Staples suggests, it seems as though those of us in the Holiness tradition have not made this connection.[10] However, it is now being recognized historically that at the close of revivals and camp meetings across the country in the nineteenth century, Communion was often served. Perhaps these Holiness prescribers were not as disconnected from Wesley's understanding of the sacrament of sanctification as previously assumed. Either way, a renewed focus on the Eucharist is needed as we preach holiness in the twenty-first century, for it is a vital means of progressive sanctification and growth in grace.[11]

9. For a full treatment of how Wesley interpreted the Eucharist, see Staples, *Outward Sign and Inward Grace*, and Ole E. Borgen, *John Wesley on the Sacraments* (Grand Rapids: Zondervan, 1985). I interpret Wesley as between the theory of spiritual presence and the memorialist view. Key to interpreting Wesley's understanding of Communion is his pneumatology. I am not sure these connections have been explored to the fullest.

10. Staples, "Things Shakeable and Things Unshakeable in Holiness Theology," The Edwin Crawford Lecture, Northwest Nazarene University's Wesley Conference: *Revisioning Holiness*, February 9, 2007. See nnu.edu/Wesley.

11. For more, see Diane Leclerc, "Steward of the Sacraments" in Al Truesdale, ed., *The Pastor as Theological Steward* (Kansas City, MO: The Foundry Publishing, 2022), 90–105.

EIGHT

Fulfilling our Purpose
Floyd Cunningham

Bless the God and Father of our Lord Jesus Christ! He has blessed us in Christ with every spiritual blessing that comes from heaven. God chose us in Christ to be holy and blameless in God's presence before the creation of the world. God destined us to be his adopted children through Jesus Christ because of his love. This was according to his goodwill and plan and to honor his glorious grace that he has given to us freely through the Son whom he loves. We have been ransomed through his Son's blood, and we have forgiveness for our failures based on his overflowing grace, which he poured over us with wisdom and understanding. God revealed his hidden design to us, which is according to his goodwill and the plan that he intended to accomplish through his Son. This is what God planned for the climax of all times: to bring all things together in Christ, the things in heaven along with the things on earth. We have also received an inheritance in Christ. We were destined by the plan of God, who accomplishes everything according to his design. We are called to be an honor to God's glory because we were the first to hope in Christ. You too heard the word of truth in Christ, which is the good news of your salvation. You were sealed with the promised Holy Spirit because you believed in Christ. The Holy Spirit is the down payment on our inheritance, which is applied toward our redemption as God's own people, resulting in the honor of God's glory.

—Ephesians 1:3–14 (CEB)

One of the most important ways of talking about the sanctified life is to speak of fulfilling our purpose—the purpose for which God created us to begin with. For Wesleyan-Holiness theology, that purpose is what we call "perfect love."

To illustrate, an old farmer in Southeast Asia bragged to the other farmers in the village, "I have the perfect water buffalo." He meant that, when he placed the yoke on the water buffalo and took him to plow in the rice field, the water buffalo perfectly pulled the plow that dug deeply into the muddy field in order to prepare it for planting rice. The old farmer thought surely that was the purpose for which God created water buffaloes.

The same farmer bragged again to the other farmers in the village, "I have the perfect hen." He meant that, each morning when he looked underneath the hen, he found an egg. Sometimes two. It seemed to him that certainly that was what God intended hens to do.

The old farmer did not attempt to place a yoke on the hen, or lead it to the muddy rice fields to plow. Yet he thought he had the perfect hen. Neither, when he went to fetch the water buffalo each morning in order to take the beast to the muddy fields, did he peer underneath where the water buffalo had lain and expect to find an egg or two. Yet he believed he had the perfect water buffalo.

The same farmer bragged once more to the other farmers in the village, "I have the perfect wife." Now what did he mean? He had not forlornly looked each morning where she slept to see if she might have, perchance, laid an egg or two. He did not place a yoke on her neck and lead her into the mud to plow the rice fields. Did he mean that she swept the simple farmhouse where they lived and kept it as clean as she could? Did he mean that she rarely burned the rice? Or that she managed to grow a few vegetables for them to eat? No. He bragged, "I have the perfect wife" because, somehow, after all the years they had been married, amid the meager life they lived together, when he came home from the fields, sweaty, his hands gnarled, his toes permanently bent and twisted from balancing himself across the narrow ledges separating the rice paddies, his face etched deeply with wrinkles, somehow, she loved him.

What could "perfect" mean? We could think of God's perfection as omniscience. Would Jesus have meant for us to be all-knowing as God is all-knowing? No matter if we study day and night until Jesus comes again, we would not measure a fraction of what God knows. Did he mean for us to be omnipotent as God is omnipotent? Was he beckoning us toward miraculous, supernatural strength? Unlikely. Omnipresence? Absurd.

Jesus was not thinking in these terms. Both Matthew 5:48 and 19:21 use the word *teleis*, which Matthew's primarily Hebrew readers understood as fulfillment, or the completeness, of one's essential nature—which, in God's case, as they well knew, is faithful, covenantal love. God's own *completeness* is love. Luke helpfully translated what Jesus said as "merciful": *be merciful as God is merciful* (see 6:36). That makes sense. Even Matthew 5:48 indicates by its preceding context that God's perfection is evident in love toward all, including those who hate and persecute and who, for whatever reason, cannot love in return. Furthermore, Jesus pushes us to love our enemies as well as our neighbors. God causes the sun to shine on the evil and the good, and rain to fall on both. Sometimes the rain is good; other times, in excess, it is bad; either way, God does not show favoritism—unlike us. Sometimes we do good things because we want a reward. We easily love those who love us and who are able to love us in return. We greet our brothers and sisters who are like us. Not much grace is needed for that. Even unbelievers do that. What differentiates us? Greeting those who are *not* our sisters or brothers, loving *enemies*, praying for those who *persecute* us. The ability to love differentiates us as human beings created in God's image. And the Godlike character of our love differentiates us from others.

"Right belief" is not an outward sign
of inward grace.

Does this background help when we turn to Matthew 19 and the rich man? During the time of Jesus, the keeping of the law—particularly the commandments but also the additional laws added across the generations—was considered to be a sufficient indicator of eternal life. Why, then, was the rich man looking beyond what he was already doing to inherit eternal life? He must have sensed his lack of something; he must have been dissatisfied with the sufficiency of morality, or at least with the standards of morality he lived by. Why was he dissatisfied? Why had keeping the law not given him assurance of his salvation? Why did he turn to Jesus—of all the rabbis he might have turned to—asking what he might do to inherit eternal life? Was there something he saw in Jesus's life that he recognized as different from the other rabbis? Something in Jesus's teaching? Something in his goodness that transcended the goodness of other rabbis? Some God-given quality within Jesus that was different from the Pharisees?

Jesus also said, "Unless your righteousness surpasses that of the Pharisees and the teachers of the law, you will certainly not enter the kingdom of heaven" (Matthew 5:20). Perhaps the rich man had heard this and wondered, what was that one thing—maybe that one law beyond the multitude of laws the Pharisees and teachers of the law taught—that, if he did it, might assure him entry into the kingdom of heaven?

In the days between his triumphal entry and his crucifixion, Jesus laid into the Pharisees and teachers of the law in his harshest rebukes (see Matthew 23). They do not practice what they preach, Jesus said. They tie heavy burdens of the law upon the shoulders of others, but they themselves do not follow what they are teaching or "lift a finger" to help (v. 4). Everything they do is for others to see. They want places of honor and to have people recognize them and greet them with respect. The Pharisees and teachers of the law are "blind guides" (v. 16) They tithe down to the littlest seed but lack justice, mercy, and faithfulness. Outside they look really good, but inside, there is greed and self-indulgence, hypocrisy and wickedness. In his upside-down way of looking at things, Jesus called these very righteous-looking religious leaders a "brood of vipers" (v. 33).

So it was not just one more good thing, that one outward sign, that the rich man could have added to the Pharisees' and teachers' supposed righteousness to bring himself assurance of eternal life. It was a matter of the heart—a heart emptied of greed, self-indulgence, hypocrisy, and wickedness, and filled with a passion for justice, mercy, and faithfulness. Would the rich man choose to have a heart emptied of his own pride and filled with compassion for others—a heart so emptied that he would give, as an outward sign of a new life, his riches for the poor, and follow Jesus?

The rich man would have been a prized catch for any rabbi—a good follower, a good disciple. Principled, moral, righteous . . . and rich. Jesus asked for the man's self-examination. The commands Jesus recited to the young man are relational and reciprocal. They are the "do unto others as you would have them do unto you" commands. We would not want our neighbor to murder us, to commit adultery with our spouse, to steal from us, or to give false testimony about us. We would want to be honored by our children.

According to the rich man, he had obeyed all the commandments. He was faultless. He was *good*. But Jesus beckoned him toward something beyond goodness, to another stage of religious development: perfection. To be *perfect* means becoming what we are created to be. We were created in God's image, and God's image is love, so we were created *for* love. Reflecting God's image of love looks like reaching out to those who need love, especially those who are abused and overlooked by others, and those different from ourselves. To be perfect is to be in the process of be-coming (not attaining in a complete sense, as Paul wrote of himself to the Philippians in 3:12–14) what we were created to be: persons of selfless love.

The rich man had more than enough and had lived righteously by all of the rules of his community. Jesus did not ask him to follow more rules or to affirm the right beliefs. For some, right belief is everything. Yet one might memorize great swaths of Scripture and have memorized a catechism but not have love—or even Christ—in their hearts. Jesus said it himself: "You study the Scriptures diligently because you think that in them you have eternal life. These are the very Scriptures that testify about me, yet you refuse to come to me to have life" (John 5:39–40). Only a generation after the great Reformers Martin Luther and John Calvin, many had reduced faith to *belief*, and had made belief into intellectual assent to creeds and cate-chisms. To be a Christian was to be baptized and to grow up understanding and affirming the faith.

The Anabaptists objected to this trend and organized what they called "believers' churches" made up of those who, as adults, had voluntarily repented and believed, and who were then baptized. Similarly, the seventeenth-century Pietists stressed the importance of heart religion—an expe-riential faith. In the eighteenth century, Jonathan Edwards called his members, all of whom had been baptized as children and raised in the church, to repent and have faith. He was voted out as pastor of his church in Northamp-ton, Massachusetts. At the same time, rather scandalously, Wesley said we should not be surprised to see heretics in heaven, and many teachers of religion *not* make it there. He himself experienced a significant change in what we now call his "Aldersgate experience," which is when he under-stood salvation by faith alone for himself.

In the nineteenth century, the evangelists also called those who had been baptized—those who had been raised in Sunday schools and who might be masters of doctrine—to repent and have faith; to be born again. In any century, it was a great affront to tell settled Christians they needed to be born again. Like other churches arising in the nineteenth century, the Holiness churches were "believers' churches." Membership in the fledgling Holiness denominations was not based on anything (not even baptism) except being born again, and on one's covenanting to follow the wisdom of the church while pursuing holiness.

"Right belief" is not an outward sign of inward grace. In the early twentieth century, we see the supposed differences between science and religion come to a head. Without a lengthy introduction to the history of fundamentalism early in the century, may it suffice to say that it became very important to a faction of Christianity to write down "fundamental" statements as a litmus test of whether a person was a good Christian. What this did was turn Christianity from an experiential, living faith that works itself out in love into a set of propositions to be affirmed. It has been made clear elsewhere (Al Truesdale's *Square Peg*, for example) that Holiness denominations do not affirm a majority of these statements. It is unfortunate that some in the Holiness tradition do not know we are not fundamentalists. When a set of propositional statements defines Christian faith, something vital is lost. If you ask Wesley and his successors what it means to be Christian, they will not answer with belief statements. They will answer something like, "Is your faith filled with the energy of love?"

Although right confession of faith—a correct understanding of Scripture, creeds, and councils—would be an outward sign of inward grace to some, it has never been sufficient for the Wesleyan-Holiness tradition. When Jesus beckoned, "If you want to be perfect" (Matthew 19:21), he was not talking about right understanding of his own teachings. He was talking about following him. He was talking about discipleship. He was calling the rich man to be perfected in love. Perfect? That is—if you want to be fulfilled, if you want to be truly joyful, if you want to be the person God created you to be—do as I have done and leave everything behind. "Sell your possessions and give to the poor, and you will have treasure in heaven. Then come, follow me" (v. 21). Jesus was asking for a radical act of *agape, kenotic* (self-giving) love. Jesus knew following this command would give this man joy and fulfillment. Instead, the rich man chose himself over others, and went away sad.

Jesus did not say to the rich man, "Accept me," or even, "Believe in me," but, "Follow me." Live like I live, see the world as I see the world, see the suffering and poverty of others as I see the suffering and poverty of others. Be my disciple—that is the invitation. The invitation is to holiness. What is it to be holy in keeping the law but not belong to God, supremely, totally, today?

The rich man heard it: *leave everything and come, follow me.* But he chose not to belong to God through Jesus. Instead, he chose to belong to his riches. Riches were his ultimate concern, and he made of them an idol, deposing God from rightful supremacy in his life. His riches isolated him from the poor. Holiness brings into our lives a capacity for relationship with God and others. Holiness offers true and full humanity. Holiness offers community with God, with other disciples, and with the poor. The rich man turned away from community because community lived out in fellowship with the poor would have required too much. He made his choice. He remained absorbed in himself, more interested in retaining riches than in relationships. No wonder he went away sad—for, by choosing riches over relationships, he withdrew from his own humanity.

Then Jesus turned to the disciples and declared how hard it is for the rich to enter the kingdom of God. The disciples had already done what Jesus told the rich man to do; they had left everything, including their livelihoods, to follow him. But they were still surprised because, just like some still think today, riches were seen as a sign of God's favor, an external sign of God's blessing. To view riches as the blessing of God is dangerous reasoning that goes against Scripture—think of the book of Job, for instance. It is wrong to believe that the poor are condemned and predestined by God to that station in life. It is wrong to conclude they are poor because they are sinful or slothful. Yet that was what many people thought in Jesus's day, and it is what many think today—which is why it was so surprising for Jesus to say how hard it is for the *rich* to enter the kingdom of God. Jesus's heart went out to the poor. Whatever our idol may be—whether money or something else—when we attend to it over our call to follow Christ sacrificially, we hurt ourselves in the process. We cannot find true human fulfillment when something other than God is our god. Period.

Wesley's message was radical for the same reason. In his own time, the Church of England was patronized by the gentry class, who cared nothing for the welfare or faith of the people in the lower classes. The common people were baptized, married, and buried by the church, but who cared for the rough and uncouth rabble in the periods between those major life stages? The rich decided they were privileged and predestined by God, so the poor must simply accept their station in life; the order of the world was as God intended it to be, and the poor were among the damned. Wesley, however, preached to the poor about the democracy of God's grace that reached even them. He visited the poor and urged his followers to do the same. They were not poor because they were sinful or lazy, Wesley insisted, but because of the social system that kept the rich,

No wonder he went away sad—for,
by choosing riches over relationships,
he withdrew from his own humanity.

rich. And how hard it was—and is—for the rich to enter the kingdom of God! Wesley reversed the class-oriented way of thinking that dominated his culture—that being poor was a sign of God's damnation and being rich a sign of God's favor. The poor did not, and do not, deserve their poverty any more than the rich deserved their riches. Like Jesus, Wesley warned that being rich was *not* a sign of being in the kingdom. It is harder for a camel to go through the eye of a needle than for a rich man to enter heaven, said Jesus!

Long ago, the early church father Origen commented on the scripture about the rich man asking Jesus about eternal life. Origen asked about the man: if he claimed to have followed all the commands—including the one to love one's neighbor as oneself—then why was he still so rich and his neighbors still so poor? A millennium after Origen, Francis of Assisi heard the same biblical story and took it literally. He tore off the finery of his father, rejected the social hierarchies that dominated the church in his day, and did what Jesus asked, and what Wesley would later do, and took the gospel to the poor. To live with them, suffer with them, understand them, and demonstrate love to them, he had to become one of them. Francis of Assisi's zeal redefined holiness for the other religious orders, which had grown rich. They had built magnificent, ostentatious monasteries that separated them from the poor and also separated them from their monastic calling to poverty as well as chastity and obedience. The Franciscans went out of the cloistered life into the villages, carrying with them the message of the gospel, expressed more by the simple, Christlike way they lived than by the sermons they preached.

Following in the same path came Francis Asbury. Upon hearing Wesley's call for missionaries to the British colonies in North America, he offered himself, never returning to England. Asbury lived an itinerant life in the new land, with no residence to call his own. This first bishop of American

Methodism possessed nothing he could not carry in his saddlebags. He begrudgingly accepted a new set of clothes from those he served, who had noticed how worn and tattered his garments were and felt embarrassed that their bishop would dress more like a beggar than a cleric. Asbury did not live like this to attain his own salvation. Neither did he live simply for its own sake. He lived according to the purpose to which God had called him, which is to say he was living teleologically, for the sake of others. After Asbury, the nineteenth-century Holiness Movement beckoned all Methodists to live for the sake of others—to live out a social agenda for the enslaved, for women and children, for the poor and downtrodden. Sanctifying grace compelled them toward "the least of these" (see Matthew 25:40).

Did Jesus really intend what he said to the rich man to be a command for everyone, everywhere? For everyone, everywhere to sell all their possessions and give them to the poor? *No*, we rationalize, *certainly not*. Perhaps we are in peril not to take Jesus's words more literally than we often have in the course of Christian history. It would be much easier if the path to Christian perfection were a confirmation liturgy, a prayer for sanctifying grace at an altar, a commitment to giving up vices or bad habits, or some other tangible way to evaluate our sanctification. Is living simply, simply for the sake of others, too much to ask? This is holiness: we are invited to enter into a way of life; not simply to make a decision regarding the lordship of Christ in an abstract or spiritual way but to live for him as his fully consecrated and surrendered disciples in every area of our lives.

There was another man—a contemporary of the rich man who was, if not equally wealthy, perhaps more intellectual, and equally filled with moral pride. Like the rich man, he put confidence in the flesh. Circumcised on the eighth day, he called himself a "Hebrew of Hebrews" (Philippians 3:5). If the rich man had kept the law from his youth, this man had done so even more. He was a Pharisee. As far as righteousness under the law, both this man and the rich man could find each other faultless. This man met Jesus not through rabbinic discourse but on the road to Damascus. Like the rich man, he was at a crossroads, but unlike the rich man, he decided to give up everything—even if it cost him his life—to follow Jesus. The laws—the good things the rich man was living by and searching for—Paul came to view as rubbish (see Philippians 3:8). He voluntarily lost all things for the sake of gaining Christ. He came to yearn after the righteousness that comes from God, by faith.

To the Philippians, Paul wrote that he had not already attained perfection but that he pressed on "to take hold of that for which Christ Jesus took hold of me" (3:12)—in other words, to apprehend that for which he had been apprehended, to grasp that for which he had been grasped, to catch that for which he had been caught. That is to say, he was still in process. The sanctifying grace filling him day by day took him on an incredible journey of suffering, pain, joy, sorrow, and, through it all, no matter what, contentment (see Philippians 4:10–13).

For what purpose did God choose Paul? It was clear to Paul: "to open [the gentiles'] eyes and turn them from darkness to light, and from the power of Satan to God, so that they may receive forgiveness of sins and a place among those who are sanctified by faith in [Jesus]" (Acts 26:18). To what purpose has God called us? To reflect God's image. To love and be loved.

In his autobiography, *A Song of Ascents*, the prolific Methodist missionary to India E. Stanley Jones wrote, "I say 'what God is making of me,' for the best that I can say about myself is that I'm a Christian-in-the-making. Not yet 'made' but only in the making at eighty-three. And I'm glad I'm not 'made,' for there is joy and anticipation in *being* made. I have been ascending, am ascending, and shall ever be ascending."[1] At significant points in his life, Jones made decisions, laying out his life plans before Christ and consecrating all to him, as described in his autobiography. For what purpose did God choose E. Stanley Jones? To preach Christ to the learned Brahmin scoffers of India.

Hauntingly, Quaker sociologist Parker Palmer says, "I can't think of a sadder way to die than with the knowledge that I never showed up in this world as who I really am."[2] Jesus is calling us to live outwardly according to the inner purpose, the inner being, the inner person—the person we were created to be. The person who has stripped away false fronts and masks. A person living authentically. A person living lovingly. We might say that is holiness. When he comes to the end, Palmer says, "I'll be asking if I was faithful to my gifts, to the needs I saw around me, and to the ways I engaged those needs with my gifts—faithful, that is, to the value, rightness, and truth of offering the world the best I had, as best I could."[3] If the rich man came to the end of his life without ever having changed, could he say this of himself—that he engaged the needs of those around him with the gifts God had given him?

One cannot but feel even more sorrow for the rich man who turned away joy and fulfillment for a life of riches and sadness. Jesus knew him better than he knew himself. What Jesus beckoned this rich man to was a life of the called; depending upon God's grace, he could pursue the highest, the loftiest of goals, the fulfillment of his own purpose and being, perfection in love—which meant truly, indeed, loving others as himself. It all comes back to love. To

1. E. Stanley Jones, *A Song of Ascents: A Spiritual Autobiography* (Nashville: Abingdon, 1968), 17.

2. Parker J. Palmer, *On the Brink of Everything: Grace, Gravity, and Getting Old* (Oakland, CA: Berrett-Koehler, 2018), 176.

3. Palmer, *On the Brink of Everything*, 70–71.

say that we are created in the image of God is to say that we were created to embody love. In our own unique way, on our own unique journey, holiness is still Christlikeness.

Becoming like Christ is the aim for all of us as we seek to be what God has created, intended, and gifted us to be. We assess our progress by measuring ourselves to the human being God created us to be, not by measuring ourselves against others. Parker Palmer relates this story: "Before he died, Rabbi Zusya said: 'In the world to come they will not ask me, "Why were you not Moses?" They will ask me, "Why were you not Zusya?"'"[4] The measure is not to the expectations of others, not to the saints, no matter how saintly, but: how have we lived out our call? To be like Christ is our "one deep, supreme desire," according to a hymn that continues, "To this I fervently aspire—that I may be like Jesus. I want my heart his throne to be, so that a watching world may see his likeness shining forth in me. I want to be like Jesus."[5] One would hope this to be true of us.

Leslie Parrott was president of Eastern Nazarene College in the mid-1970s. Students considered him a great preacher. If he was scheduled to preach, they were rarely absent. He reached into the hearts of the students' needs. Parrott was to preach one summer Sunday morning at the Wollaston College Church. However, the service went long. The teens had come back from a youth camp with songs and testimonies. All good. But it was 11:55 when Dr. Parrott had the opportunity to preach, and the service was usually supposed to finish by noon. Yes, the cafeteria would open in five minutes, but the congregation would have willingly stayed—he was that good a preacher. But he preached only five minutes on: "Holiness: What Difference Does It Make?"

---

4. Palmer, *On the Brink of Everything*, 75.

5. Thomas Chisholm, "I Want to Be Like Jesus," *Sing to the Lord: Hymnal* (Kansas City, MO: Lillenas, 1993), 208.

He must have asked that question ten times or more in those five minutes. What difference does holiness make in your relationship with your spouse? What difference does holiness make in your relationship with your children or parents? What difference does holiness make in how you relate to your roommate? What difference does holiness make in your speech, in the words you use, in your attitude?

What difference does holiness make? If it doesn't mean being like Jesus, we have missed the whole point.

Embodying Holiness
Floyd Cunningham

NINE

Just as a body, though one, has many parts, but all its many parts form one body, so it is with Christ. For we were all baptized by one Spirit so as to form one body—whether Jews or Gentiles, slave or free—and we were all given the one Spirit to drink. Even so the body is not made up of one part but of many. Now if the foot should say, "Because I am not a hand, I do not belong to the body," it would not for that reason stop being part of the body. And if the ear should say, "Because I am not an eye, I do not belong to the body," it would not for that reason stop being part of the body. If the whole body were an eye, where would the sense of hearing be? If the whole body were an ear, where would the sense of smell be? But in fact God has placed the parts in the body, every one of them, just as he wanted them to be. If they were all one part, where would the body be? As it is, there are many parts, but one body. The eye cannot say to the hand, "I don't need you!" And the head cannot say to the feet, "I don't need you!" On the contrary, those parts of the body that seem to be weaker are indispensable, and the parts that we think are less honorable we treat with special honor. And the parts that are unpresentable are treated with special modesty, while our presentable parts need no special treatment. But God has put the body together, giving greater honor to the parts that lacked it, so that there should be no division in the body, but that its parts should have equal concern for each other. If one part suffers, every part suffers with it; if one part is honored, every part rejoices with it.

—1 Corinthians 12:12–26

Christian perfection is our aim.

What is this perfection? Love.

What does love look like? How is love embodied? Look at Christ.

Perfection is love, and love is God in Christ.

This life was never meant to be lived alone. Love is to be embodied by the church because we are the body of Christ. Collectively, we have the capacity to be more like Christ than we do individually. Collectively, we are more loving than we are individually. Jesus invited the rich man from a life of solitary and lonely individualism into community with his disciples; he invited the rich man to live in fellowship with him; *and* he invited the rich man into a fellowship of love with those to whom he would give his possessions. He invited the rich man into a community of love.

When we join the band of Christ's disciples, we are *embodied*—incorporated into a fellowship that walks together, talks about Christ together, and experiences transforming grace together. We have discussed what holiness looks like in the life of an individual disciple. We now turn to what we call "corporate holiness."

Charlie was an active, eleven-year old boy with high-support-needs autism. His parents had been thinking about attending church. They decided it was time to try to find a congregation that would love them and love their son. About halfway through Sunday school one morning, Charlie's parents were summoned. The volunteers couldn't handle him. They were asked to find another church because this church "couldn't meet his needs." Other churches conveyed the same sentiment. The family finally gave up and decided that attending church was too hard.

We all know people who have been hurt by the church—people who have been so offended, wounded, or even abused that they've given up. Perhaps you've had this experience yourself. Church is sometimes dysfunctional, uncomfortable, cross-purposed, and painful. We have pastors who fail God, themselves, and their congregations. We endure grumpy, self-righteous criticism in the walls of the church. We fight each other—sometimes to the point of parting ways for good. Some observers say we are in danger of losing a whole generation of embittered souls who believe the church has lost its relevance and neglected their needs.

Yet we continue to call the church "holy." According to the Nicene Creed, the church has four classical marks: "one, holy, catholic, and apostolic." We confess that the church is formed through the Holy Spirit and participates in God's own holiness. Sometimes we call it the "spotted bride" of Christ. Other times we proclaim, in the words of a nineteenth-century hymn, that it is a "glorious church, without spot or wrinkle."[1] How do we explain the seeming contradiction between what we *believe about* the church and what we *experience in* the church? Is it wishful thinking to proclaim the church holy? Are pain and heartache inevitable?

If there were ever a dysfunctional church, it was the church at Corinth. Paul's first letter to the Corinthians reads like a laundry list of problems. Every chapter presents at least one issue where the church is missing the mark. There are scandals, disagreements, confusion, and outright sin. Members quarrel, pridefully taking sides against one another. They hurt and alienate one another. Yet, at the very beginning of the first letter, Paul addresses members as those who are sanctified in Christ Jesus and called to be saints. Despite their failures, Paul does not forget what Christ can do in and through them. He points them to their God-enabled potential. In a sense, Paul tells them: *You are holy. Now become who you are.* How can the Corinthian church be both holy and not holy?

1. Ralph E. Hudson, "A Glorious Church," *Sing to the Lord*, 672.

One way to explain this paradox is through the concept of Christ's "imputed righteousness." We usually apply this to individuals, but it also applies to the church corporate. To have Christ's righteousness imputed to us means it belongs to us and counts in our favor. It means having his righteousness cover over our sinfulness so God can perceive us as righteous even though we aren't. Even though we lack any holiness of our own, we are clothed in the white robe of Christ's holiness. To claim that the church can enjoy imputed righteousness is not to ignore its failings and shortcomings, but it does remind us of an important aspect of holiness: it is derived from another source.

Human beings derive our holiness from the unique holiness of God. So does the church as a whole. "I am the LORD, who makes you holy," God says in Exodus (31:13) and Leviticus (22:32). Leviticus has numerous other references to God's holiness:

> "I am the LORD your God; consecrate yourselves and be holy, because I am holy. . . . I am the LORD, who brought you up out of Egypt to be your God; therefore, be holy, because I am holy" (11:44–45).

> "Consecrate yourselves and be holy, because I am the LORD your God" (20:7).

> "You are to be holy to me because I, the LORD, am holy, and I have set you apart from the nations to be my own" (20:26).

Scripture shows a connection between God's holiness and our holiness that must not be forgotten. Our holiness is derived *from* relationship with God. Wesleyan theologian David Thompson writes:

> Characteristically in the Old Testament, holy describes someone or something in a defined relationship. Someone or something has been separated from the profane

or the unclean to specific relationship with God. . . . What is described relationally on the one hand as holy (separate) or on the other as profane/common is described ritually as clean or unclean. Thus, in these contexts clean and unclean do not substantially describe the condition of the person or thing, but characterize it with respect to its relationship to the divine. To be clean in this sense is to be holy—set in relation to God; to be unclean is to be unholy—out of and unfit for relation to the divine. In either case, the point is proper or improper relation to God.[2]

Even in a church full of surrendered believers, human frailty alone will lead to problems. But many problems in the church are caused by sin, and we are never told to stay put in our sin. Paul expected the Corinthian church to change and grow. God expects the same progress in our churches today. Yes, the church is holy because God, on the basis of Christ's imputed righteousness, proclaims it so. But if we desire to move beyond being *called* holy—if we desire to *be* holy—then we must cooperate with such grace. In this sense, the holiness of the church is dependent on the holiness of its people. Always and forever, the holiness of its people is dependent on the sanctifying grace of God, who is in essence holy love. The church is God's church. May God help us become who we are.

Distractions and Detractors from Community

Talking about what goes wrong in church is difficult. It is a topic that often goes underground where it can be ignored. It is not as if most of our members *intend* to spread viciousness and treat others poorly. But in light of the great numbers of people today who express church hurt, and are

---

2. David Thompson, "Old Testament Bases of the Wesleyan Message" *Wesleyan Theological Journal* 10 (1975): 39.

leaving because of it, it is not something we can overlook. Consider the following descriptions of dysfunction.

1. Deprecation

Damage is done to the church when there is *deprecation* of different viewpoints. The oft-quoted saying is extremely relevant here: "In essentials, unity; in nonessentials, liberty; in all things, charity [love]."[3]

Wesley's sentiments on this point are most readily found in the sermon "Catholic Spirit." He was preaching on how we handle different viewpoints among Christians without it hindering our ability to love them. He said a "catholic spirit" is the key, by which he meant the ability to think and let think on nonessentials. Love must be over all we do, even in our theological and practical disagreements.

If you asked Wesley (and, hopefully, Wesleyans) what it means to be Christian, the answer would not affirm certain theological statements. Wesley wanted to know the quality of our love for others. There was essential theology that was still important to him; he knew what he believed on every point—but love was the ultimate answer to the question of what it means to be Christian.

Complicating the problem today is that Christians disagree on what is essential and what is not. Since we are still not far removed from modernism, conceptual disagreements even between Christians can lead to demonizing those with other viewpoints to the point that it eliminates the possibility of respectful dialogue. This issue is problematic inside a local church, on a denominational level, and at the ecumenical level.

Holiness calls us to more.

---

3. Rupertus Meldenius is probably the person who said this, although it has been attributed to Augustine, Wesley, and even Phineas Bresee.

2. Dehumanization and Depersonalization

In order to disagree without guilt around how we treat others, it is incredibly tempting to *dehumanize* or *depersonalize* one another. It is then easier to attack the other person's character. Attacking someone's personhood is a common way to discredit their position, instead of engaging with what they say or think.

We treat others as objects instead of subjects loved by God. We forget that everyone is created in the image of God. We forget that each of us has a story and life experiences that have shaped us. When we de-*person*-alize others, we define people based on one event or encounter, or we generalize people, erasing their uniqueness.

We generalize groups of people and use unflattering labels. We use "us" and "them" language that is inherently polarizing. We forget to see people *as* people, and we forget that they are parts of the body that Paul clearly tells us we need. "The eye cannot say to the hand, 'I don't need you!'" (1 Corinthians 12:21).

Holiness calls us to more.

3. Demoralization

Another type of church dysfunction comes through *demoralization*, which leads to the nasty habit of looking for someone to blame. Certainly, local churches and denominations go through periods of time that are painful and discouraging. Unfortunately, that can be the time when we splinter into factions and begin finger-pointing. Our pain must be someone's fault, we reason. But even if there is a person as a root cause, we are called to encourage a weaker brother or sister or to confront the situation directly and compassionately. When we splinter, we start to disintegrate.

We also can isolate ourselves as a means of self-protection. When we are demoralized at church, we lose energy to contribute our time for the betterment of the whole. We begin to live into the world's individualism. We become obsessed with our own pet peeves. At our worst, we turn to the use of deception, rumor-spreading, and even name-calling.

Holiness calls us to so much more!

In 1 Corinthians 12, Paul outlined how a holy church should function. And, of course, chapter 12 is followed by chapter 13, the grand love chapter. Paul implied that all the problems he had addressed up to this point would work themselves out if only love reigned as it ought. Wesley asked, "Is your faith filled with the energy of love?" If we are as a church in a proper relationship with God through Christ, righteousness is given to us collectively. Still, we need to be honest that the church today remains far from what it is called to be. Is this all we can expect—to continue failing and merely allowing God's righteousness to cover us? Or is there something more?

In our tradition, our holiness goes further, even collectively. Not only are we *perceived* as holy by God because of Christ's righteousness, but God also seeks to remake us as *truly* holy, to change us from sinners to saints who live in *holy* communion with one another. God first declares us holy but then gradually imparts the holiness that enables us to become who we are *as the church*. We really are transformed from the inside out. The theologically technical way of talking about this is that *imputed* righteousness must be followed with *imparted* righteousness.

It is important to distinguish between true and false meanings of holiness. It is very easy, for instance, to equate holiness with avoiding sinful acts, but this was the underlying disagreement between Jesus and some of the Pharisees, who attempted to follow religious laws perfectly. Jesus pointed out again and again that what matters most is the condition of the heart. They could technically call themselves faultless (as Paul does in Philippians) yet fall short of what Christ values most: a life of loving relationships. Holiness is never a passive condition of having abstained from certain wrongs. It requires the purposeful desire to walk rightly in love—an active, engaged, embodied love for God, one another, and the world. In the context of the church, holiness means living out this call of love in relation to one another.

The Church's Holy Purpose

It is good to be reminded and grounded in why God created the church to begin with.

First, the church's purpose is to represent Christ on earth. We become the body of Christ in his bodily absence. We are to go where Christ would go and do the ministry Christ would do. We are to share the good news that Jesus Christ can save and redeem, sanctify and make whole, give persons purpose and meaning, and give them a people called the church to incorporate and embrace them.

Embodied holiness compels collective witness. Missiologists as well as historians have prodded evangelicals into thinking about corporate movements toward Christ. We could cook rice one grain at a time, or we could cook rice all together in one large, steaming pot. Or, to change the metaphor, we could fish with one fishing pole, or we could fish with a net. Early in Christian history, whole kingdoms became Christian at the will of a ruler. During the Reformation whole countries became Protestant. Catechism and revival followed. More recently, in places like India, whole villages, led by chiefs and elders, decided to become Christian. Discipleship followed. We must not dismiss such movements as shallow.

In the Philippines, visiting U.S. evangelists are pleasantly surprised to see whole congregations come forward to the altar after they preach. The congregation is exhorted to respond to the message, and they respond as a corporate whole, submitting in spiritual worship to the Word of God. It seems wise to invite families and groups toward collective repentance, to collectively seek God's forgiveness, since each person is part of a group and responds within it. After Peter's sermon at Pentecost, an entire group of people joined the church by accepting Christ, and "and about three thousand were added to their number that day" (Acts 2:41).

Look at Ephesians 3:14–19 from a group perspective: that Christ may dwell in our *collective* hearts by faith; that we *together, corporately,* may be rooted and established in love, that we *together* may have power—*together with all the saints*—to grasp how wide and long and high and deep is the love of Christ, and to be *together* as his people, as his church, as his children, filled to the measure of all of the fullness of God.

We are also to minister to the poor, the outcast, the stranger, and the vulnerable. We are to feed them, invite them in, heal them, and show hospitality to them. Our hearts are cleansed by God, which impels us, as the church, to get our feet dirty in the world's messiness. If the church is to be holy, it must fulfill its ultimate purpose as Christ's body—to re-present Christ to the world—not reluctantly but with outstretched hands.

Second, the church is meant to fulfill its purpose by living in a vital, interdependent way with one another. There is no individualism in the body, no such thing as a solitary Christian. The ear or eye cannot say of another part, "I don't need you." Rather, every part of the body needs every other part if the body is to fulfill its purpose on earth. Although we are called to love the whole world, there is a particular love we owe to our brothers and sisters in Christ. Wesley said we are to love fellow believers more than we love people of the world. He also told us specifically what that looks like: praying for one another and spurring each other on to good works. Paul tells us we are

Holiness is never a passive condition of having abstained from certain wrongs. It requires the purposeful desire to walk rightly in love— an active, engaged, embodied love for God, one another, and the world.

to work together, building up the other parts of the body. When one part mourns, all mourn. When one part rejoices, all rejoice. We depend on one another when life becomes difficult. We depend on one another to lift our praises to God. We encourage and help one another. We help each part become its best self. If the church is to be holy, it must be characterized by relationships of mutual love and care.

Third, the body of Christ is called to value all of its parts in equal measure. This would have been a surprising expectation to Paul's audience. Equality was not a concept in Greco-Roman society. Everyone had a particular part to play, but it was clear who had value—who had power and authority—and who didn't in Paul's context. Paul dares to proclaim that in God's economy, the less presentable parts have equal value. Further, the disabled parts are treated with special honor. Think back to Charlie, our eleven-year-old boy with high-support-needs autism. If the church is being the church, Charlie should be honored above all others.

Because our tradition affirms that Pentecost was both the birthday of the church and its defining moment, the prophecy of Joel was fulfilled, which Peter preaches. We have therefore always affirmed that any person can hold any office in the church, including ordination and serving in the highest posts. The kingdom of God is upside down from the way the world operates. If the church is to be holy, it must affirm that every part of the body of Christ—every person—is highly valued, equally needed, and deeply loved.

We end with a case study. The church at Corinth evidenced God's saving grace to all, regardless of ethnic or religious background. Embodied holiness became an issue in relation to meat offered to idols. There was a faction in the church that was theologically right yet morally wrong. The converts from paganism were hurt by their siblings in Christ. For the former pagans, meat consecrated to idols was too much a reminder of their old ways of living and worshiping at the temples. They had given up such ways of life. Some Christian converts had no such prejudices and advocated unrestricted consumption of meat offered to idols. All things are created good, they rightly argued. No transfiguration, or transubstantiation, of meat takes place when it is offered to idols. Neither does food change our relation to God. *Let us find the correct theology of meat offered to idols and act on it*, was their way of thinking. They allowed intellect to determine their conduct and ethics—a false starting place, Paul said, that was based on pride and arrogance (see 1 Corinthians 4:18–19). Those who ate the meat were correct in their theological and religious understanding of meat, but they were absolutely morally wrong in their practice.

Eating meat is an *amoral* circumstance theologically: it does not have moral significance attached to it. It is not a great Christological issue like Paul had to address with other churches. Meat eating (or not) is not one of the essentials. There are some things worth fighting for, but this is not one. However, the roughshod use of legitimate liberty became a stumbling block for the Corinthian church. Meat eating *became* immoral because it hindered and broke personal relationships.

True knowledge does not boast. True knowledge realizes its own inadequacies. Holiness is living for others. If my eating meat disrupts my relationship with fellow Christians or causes anyone to fall, "I will never eat meat again" (8:13)! What we do must be based on our love and need for the Christian community that spiritually nourishes us. We need the community of those baptized with Christ to give us our moral bearings. By ourselves, we cannot determine the way God requires. We are too prone to rationalizing. For the sake of the community, we subordinate our individual "rights." Freedom, writes one commentator about this 1 Corinthians 8 passage, "is not a liberation from the restraints of interpersonal relationships."[4] Our aim is building up with love. Paul grounds holiness ethics not in knowledge but in *love*—which the Corinthians neglected.[5] Love is the bond among us that enables us to live in harmony. Sanctifying grace comes upon a community, not simply upon individuals. The whole point of sanctifying grace is for the community—for living in community and for the community's witness to Christ.

The point of this episode in the Corinthian church is not about eating meat; it is about living together as the people of God. It is about being humble, gentle, patient, and bearing with one another. Holiness is about making every effort to keep the unity of the Spirit through the bond of peace. Holiness is about being one body empowered by the one Spirit. Holiness is about allowing the one hope, one Lord, one faith, one baptism—the one God of us all, who is over all and through all and in all—to bind us together inseparably as one. The world is too needy for it to be otherwise among us.

---

4. Wendell Lee Willis, *Idol Meat in Corinth: The Pauline Argument in 1 Corinthians 8 and 10* (Chico, CA: Scholars Press, 1985), 115.

5. See especially J. Ayodeji Adewuya, *Holiness and Community in 2 Corinthians 6:14–7:1: Paul's View of Communal Holiness in the Corinthian Correspondence* (New York: Peter Lang, 2001).

The Journey toward the Future

Holiness and Suffering

TEN

For God, who said, "Let light shine out of darkness," made his light shine in our hearts to give us the light of the knowledge of God's glory displayed in the face of Christ. But we have this treasure in jars of clay to show that this all-surpassing power is from God and not from us. We are hard pressed on every side, but not crushed; perplexed, but not in despair; persecuted, but not abandoned; struck down, but not destroyed. We always carry around in our body the death of Jesus, so that the life of Jesus may also be revealed in our body. For we who are alive are always being given over to death for Jesus' sake, so that his life may also be revealed in our mortal body.

—2 Corinthians 4:6–11

In 1972 *A Theology of Love* was published. Although there is some disagreement today about the impact of this book by Mildred Bangs Wynkoop, many testify that this book kept them in the Wesleyan-Holiness tradition following the era during which legalist regression gripped Holiness denominations. During this period, holiness was only defined as what a person did *not* do instead of focusing on the actions we are called to do as evidence of the love God has shed abroad in the hearts of those wholly surrendered. Legalism tends to breed self-righteousness and judgmentalism and can express itself as hateful, even toward other Christians.

Wynkoop spoke of a "credibility gap" between the lives people *professed* to live and the unloving ways they *were* living. If we are to know the heart of a person by the fruit they produce, the fruit produced by legalism was mean, spiteful, and destructive. When Jesus said in the Beatitudes that those are blessed who endure persecution for his name's sake, did he mean persecution from other Christians? The history of the church is filled with instances of self-righteous legalism and rigid misunderstanding of orthodoxy that have killed in the name of Christ even those who were followers of Christ.

Wynkoop proposed a rediscovery of the *dynamic* of Wesleyan theology—the life we can lead by the Spirit that is life-giving, renewing, and filled with the energy of love. Where legalism leads to a harsh, static, stagnant, dead faith, true holiness leads to genuine righteousness that keeps love at the center of the holy life. The book's publication was a watershed moment; our hypocrisy was revealed and our misguided striving for a cold morality exposed.

The last reflection of the book seems oddly present. It is a short reflection on Wynkoop's own "controversy with Christ," as she labels it. In just a few paragraphs, she reflects on the implications of her paradigm that calls for continual growth in holiness until we die, as opposed to a theology that presses entire sanctification as a point of arrival, requiring little more than waiting for Christ's return. A theology focused on entire sanctification as arrival rather than progression brings about a *state* of *perfectionism* (rather than a *dynamic* of *perfection*). Wynkoop's implication was that Christ ever pushed her forward, never allowing rest. At first, the reader may feel as if Wynkoop is denying herself participation in the peace and joy a life of holiness brings. Instead, she is expressing—much like Paul in 2 Corinthians—what she endured to preach the gospel of Christ, what she endured as a minister and professor, what she endured by teaching the true dynamic of holiness, and even what she endured to get the book published.

Paul says:

Since we work together with him, we are also begging you not to receive the grace of God in vain. He says, *I listened to you at the right time, and I helped you on the day of salvation.* Look, now is the right time! Look, now is the day of salvation!

We don't give anyone any reason to be offended about anything so that our ministry won't be criticized. Instead, we commend ourselves as ministers of God in every way. We did this with our great endurance through problems, disasters, and stressful situations. We went through beatings, imprisonments, and riots. We experienced hard work, sleepless nights, and hunger. We displayed purity, knowledge, patience, and generosity. We served with the Holy Spirit, genuine love, telling the truth, and God's power. We carried the weapons of righteousness in our right hand and our left hand. We were treated with honor and dishonor and with verbal abuse and good evaluation. We were seen as both fake and real, as unknown and well known, as dying—and look, we are alive! We were seen as punished but not killed, as going through pain but always happy, as poor but making many rich, and as having nothing but owning everything.

Corinthians, we have spoken openly to you, and our hearts are wide open. There are no limits to the affection that we feel for you. You are the ones who placed boundaries on your affection for us. But as a fair trade—I'm talking to you like you are children—open your hearts wide too.

(2 Corinthians 6:1–13, CEB)

Paul suffered because he refused to give up his calling. He refused to sit on what he had already accomplished. The love of Christ compelled him forward, as it did Mildred

What makes us Christian in the midst of suffering is the affirmation that God's grace is sufficient for us. In the midst of pain and suffering we may doubt the sufficiency of God's grace, but it is real.

Bangs Wynkoop. She was willing to suffer and sacrifice for the theology of love, believing it was the heart, the essence, the key, the sum of all of Scripture; the vitality, the power, and the purpose of being made in the image of God. Love is holiness. Any holiness without love is a farce. For this truth, Wynkoop sacrificed and suffered. Her controversy with Christ was that she could not rest on what she had already accomplished; the love of Christ compelled her forward. She suffered even more once the book was published. How I wish she could have known that she actually succeeded in pushing Wesleyan faith forward toward healthier understandings of holiness that were desperately needed. It is important to note that Rob Staples, William Greathouse, and H. Ray Dunning, among others, also did important theological work along these same lines.

I reference Wynkoop's "controversy with Christ" for two reasons. First, of course, is that I embrace completely the theology of love as definitive of holiness. God's love for us, and our love for God, neighbor, and enemy is the essence of holiness. Second, I have my own controversy. It is my deepest desire that this chapter stand as a crucial corrective of erroneous understandings of the doctrine of Christian perfection and entire sanctification. These misunderstandings have caused much emotional damage and mental anguish among our people in the church. Thus, instead of a controversy with Christ, it might be said that I have a controversy with the church. That controversy can be summed up as this: it is truly possible to be holy and suffer at the same time; entire sanctification is not a cure-all for affliction; our call to minister to the least of these has not lessened one bit since Jesus's words left his tongue. John Wesley recognized this truth in a keen way, for he considered deeply and wrote about what Christian perfection is not.

The Damages of Criticism

It was one of those days when even the hills and the trees were as gray as a winter sky—but it was summer. The drive through the fog seemed to take forever, as did the walk from the car, and the elevator ride to the top floor. I began to smell that familiar antiseptic-mixed-with-illness odor. I had only been there a few times over the last six months, something for which I carried a deep, silent guilt. I should have been there more. But I was too angry, or sad, or confused. I'm not sure. I just knew it was too difficult to see him that way.

There were locks on the doors, so we signed in and waited. Soon the attending caretaker came, and I walked the long corridor to the main "recreational area." What an absurd name for this dark place. Would he be there, or would he be hiding in his room?

I spotted him in a chair beside the window. As usual, he did not gaze out, but down. It was hard to believe it was him. He'd lost more than sixty pounds. His skin seemed gray and lifeless. I wondered if he would understand that I had come to say goodbye.

"Hi, Dad."

No response.

I often wondered what went through his troubled mind. Did he understand that he was in the psych ward, or did he imagine, perhaps with a touch of truth, that we had imprisoned him?

The depression came on suddenly. Some said "breakdown." But if something breaks down, we anticipate it being fixed. Why was the fixing taking so long? They tried every drug. They tried every combination of drugs. If he had, in fact, lost his mind, where did it go, and why couldn't we find it?

It was his birthday, and I was about to leave for college. How do you celebrate a birthday when, every moment of every day of the last six months, this man had wanted to die? And how could I leave? How could I move five hundred miles away? How could I move on and embrace my future?

He looked at me, and tears welled up in his glazed eyes. Again, as he had done many times before, he put his face in his hands and cried. "I'm sorry, I'm sorry, I'm sorry. Please take me home."

You might wonder what started his torment. My dad, after decades at the same place, changed jobs. He was promised much! But his new boss was intensely critical and verbally abusive. So dad took a courageous step: he quit. He was in the hospital just days later.

He fought in Okinawa in World War II. He was, of course, part of what we call the "greatest generation"—the generation who made sacrifices hardly seen in U.S. history since. They were the generation who worked jobs without consideration for happiness or professional satisfaction. They worked for their families with little complaint.

I think Dad broke because he quit his job. It went against what he believed to be his duty to us. He was convinced when we visited him in the hospital that we were starving, without enough food, lacking the necessities of life. In his mind, he had shirked his responsibilities to us. It didn't matter how much we tried to reassure him. On the other hand, if we succeeded in reassuring him, would he take that to mean we didn't need him anymore? Tricky.

I applaud my father for quitting and standing up for himself. I think it was the bravest thing he ever did. But he suffered a horrible cost for protecting himself—twelve years of deep depression until he died.

Criticism. Harsh, belittling, verbal abuse. Criticism broke him. And it breaks us. There is, of course, constructive criticism, and a place for it. But we have to be in a particular kind of trusting relationship to receive even constructive criticism well. The problem is, let's be honest, it's a whole lot easier to give out criticism than to take it. Why is it so hard for us to turn it around—to recognize that if criticism hurts us, it will surely hurt the person we criticize? Great care should be taken to do necessary criticism lovingly.

Or maybe we don't care. Maybe that's the problem. Perhaps we criticize in order to hurt the other person.

We know the relationship between Paul and the Corinthians was rocky. Letters went back and forth—more than just the two we have. We find a major theme in 2 Corinthians of Paul needing to defend himself because their criticism of him was very, very harsh. Paul indicated in chapter 6 that they were like his own children. He would not turn his back on them. His heart would remain open. And he implored them to open their hearts to his love in return. But the level of criticism he received was astonishing, really.

In chapter 6, Paul addressed the damage to their relationship. He began his defense—or, to say it differently, he began commending himself to them—by reviewing everything he had suffered for the sake of Christ and for the gospel and for their sake. Included in Paul's list:

- Great trouble and distress
- Beatings
- Imprisonments
- Riots
- Hard work
- Sleepless nights
- Hunger
- Dishonor
- Bad report
- Being called an impostor
- Sorrowful
- Dying

- Poor
- Having nothing

Then he turned to his attitude and actions among them:

- Purity
- Understanding
- Patience
- Kindness
- In the Holy Spirit
- Sincere love
- Truthful
- Power in God
- Glory
- Good report
- Genuine
- Rejoicing
- Living for Christ's sake
- Making others rich yet possessing everything

Paul was describing a type of paradoxical living. Paradox is at the heart of the Christian faith and at the center of our most definitive doctrines. The very nature of Jesus Christ is paradoxical. He is fully God and fully human at the same time, not half-God and half-human, or any other combination of the two. The Trinity is paradoxical. We are monotheists who believe in one God, but we acknowledge that God has three "Persons." Jesus says paradoxically that we will gain our life if we lose it (see Matthew 10:39).

Paul described himself as having nothing yet possessing everything. What does "having nothing" imply? Christians are called to take up our crosses, deny ourselves, show hospitality to the stranger, and be willing to empty ourselves for the sake of the other. On the other hand, "possessing everything" implies having fullness in Christ, an abundance of love and spiritual gifts, true and living community, and being filled by the Spirit—to name a few. These are the fruits of giving everything and suffering for Christ's sake.

I believe in this kind of life with all of my heart. I believe in new creation and in what God can do in a life surrendered to him. But we rarely suffer *because of the cause of Christ*. Sometimes we suffer meaninglessly. Dad's suffering was not willed. He did not choose it. It was not for Christ's sake. There is suffering in this world that we do not choose, that is anything but our fault, that we do not expect, that comes at us with no real point in its back pocket. It comes in many shapes and sizes.

Dad's experience opened me to my own suffering and also to deeply consider the suffering of others. Sometimes I jokingly call myself an "exceptional theologian." What I mean by that is that I seem to be able to see those who are the exceptions—when we are having a good time, they sit in the corner and weep. Their lives do not fit our usual rules; they are exceptions to how we think life should go.

When I sent a new book off to the publisher, I decided to dedicate it to my dad. This is what the dedication says: "Dad, because of your dark night of the mind, heart, and soul I can see pain where many may not. I do not believe your depression was a gift from God, but it was a gift to me. May you continue, truly, to rest in peace."[1] Fred Craddock, a marvelous preacher and teacher of preaching, has a saying I've held in my heart for years:

> It is right that preachers be concerned that the Word of God not be hindered, but it is also right they understand that this hindrance may be caused not only by the mishandling of a text of Scripture but by a mis-

---

1. Diane Leclerc and Brent Peterson, *The Back Side of the Cross: An Atonement Theology for the Abused and Abandoned* (Eugene, OR: Cascade Books, 2022), v.

reading of the situation of the congregation. Taking the congregation out of context is as much a violation of the Word of God as taking the Scripture out of context. . . . [Pastors know] that even with carefully guarded study hours behind locked doors, the people stand around [their] desk[s] and whisper, "Remember me."[2]

My dad calls to me, *remember me.*

The Gospel and Suffering

What does the gospel look like in suffering beyond our control? What is the "everything" for those who suffer from this particular kind of "nothing"? What does salvation mean for them?

The following is from the blog of a young singer. She gained some notoriety for singing an original song on the TV competition show *America's Got Talent.* She got a golden ticket to move directly to the finals, but she ended up being too sick to go. She went by the name of Nightbirde.

I don't remember most of Autumn, because I lost my mind late in the summer and for a long time after that, I wasn't in my body. I was a lightbulb buzzing somewhere far.

After the doctor told me I was dying, and after the man I married said he didn't love me anymore, I chased a miracle in California and sixteen weeks later, I got it. The cancer was gone. But when my brain caught up with it all, something broke. I later found out that all the tragedy at once had caused a physical head trauma, and my brain was sending false signals of excruciating pain and panic.

---

2. Fred Craddock, *As One without Authority* (Nashville: Abingdon, 1987), 130, 132–33.

I spent three months propped against the wall. On nights that I could not sleep, I lay in the tub like an insect, staring at my reflection in the shower knob. I vomited until I was hollow. I rolled up under my robe on the tile. The bathroom floor became my place to hide, where I could scream and be ugly; where I could sob and spit and eventually doze off, happy to be asleep, even with my head on the toilet.

I have had cancer three times now, and I have barely passed thirty. There are times when I wonder what I must have done to deserve such a story. I fear sometimes that when I die and meet with God, that he will say I disappointed him, or offended him, or failed him. Maybe he'll say I just never learned the lesson, or that I wasn't grateful enough. But one thing I know for sure is this: *he can never say that he did not know me.*

I am God's downstairs neighbor, banging on the ceiling with a broomstick. I show up at his door every day. Sometimes with songs, sometimes with curses. Sometimes apologies, gifts, questions, demands. Sometimes I use my key under the mat to let myself in. Other times, I sulk outside until he opens the door to me himself.

I have called him a cheat and a liar, and I meant it. I have told him I wanted to die, and I meant it. Tears have become the only prayer I know. Prayers roll over my nostrils and drip down my forearms. They fall to the ground as I reach for him. These are the prayers I repeat night and day; sunrise, sunset.

Call me bitter if you want to—that's fair. Count me among the angry, the cynical, the offended, the hardened. But count me also among the friends of God. For I have seen him in rare form. I have felt his exhale,

The heart of God is present to the weak in mysterious ways we do not often understand. Yet God is not only present— God is also powerfully active.

lain in his shadow, squinted to read the message he wrote for me in the grout: "I'm sad too."

If an explanation would help, he would write me one—I know it. But maybe an explanation would only start an argument between us—and I don't want to argue with God. I want to lie in a hammock with him and trace the veins in his arms.

I remind myself that I'm praying to the God who let the Israelites stay lost for decades. They begged to arrive in the promised land, but instead he let them wander, answering prayers they didn't pray. For forty years, their shoes didn't wear out. Fire lit their path each night. Every morning, he sent them mercy-bread from heaven.

I look hard for the answers to the prayers that I didn't pray. I look for the mercy-bread that he promised to bake fresh for me each morning. The Israelites called it *manna*, which means, "what is it?"

That's the same question I'm asking—again, and again. There's mercy here somewhere—*but what is it? What is it? What is it?*

I see mercy in the dusty sunlight that outlines the trees, in my mother's crooked hands, in the blanket my friend left for me, in the harmony of the wind chimes. It's not the mercy that I asked for, but it *is* mercy nonetheless. And I learn a new prayer: *thank you.* It's a prayer I don't mean yet, but will repeat until I do.

Call me cursed, call me lost, call me scorned. But that's not all. Call me chosen, blessed, sought after. Call me the one whom God whispers his secrets to. I am the one whose belly is filled with loaves of mercy that were hidden for me.

Even on days when I'm not so sick, sometimes I go lie on the mat in the afternoon light to listen for him. I know it sounds crazy, and I can't really explain it, but God is in there—even now. I have heard it said that some people can't see God because they won't look low enough, and it's true.

If you can't see him, look lower. God is on the bathroom floor.[3]

This is the gospel too—God on the bathroom floor with us. This is salvation too—God present in the suffering. It was God's presence through the suffering for Nightbirde, whose real name was Jane. Brent Peterson and I wrote a book together on suffering that released in 2022. I knew Jane was a Christian and had gone to a Christian college. I was so moved by her words that I emailed her and got her permission to reprint this piece from her blog. She died in February 2022, only a few months after our exchange.

What we do *not* say is that her death and her suffering were good! We also do not say that God *caused* her pain and her death. What we *can* say is that God was present in every moment and in every space of her suffering. Our suffering and pain are not good. But God is present in every moment and in every space of our suffering.

Sometimes in Christianity, people connect sin directly with suffering. It is a concept found in the Old Testament and in the New Testament. It is the idea that the entire book of Job counters. Job gives us insight into how *not* to do theodicy. When Job's friends continue to challenge him to connect his suffering with his sin, he refuses to take this logical path. In the end, his friends are exposed as wrong. Yet, many centuries after the writing of this wisdom book,

_____

3. Nightbirde, "God Is on the Bathroom Floor," March 9, 2021, https://www.nightbirde.co/blog/2021/9/27/god-is-on-the-bathroom-floor.

we are still temped to take this logical path and blame suffering on the sufferer. There *is* innocent suffering in the world, beyond our ability to comprehend.

Why? we ask.

Why does suffering exist?

Where is God?

These are the questions that repeat like echoes through the centuries, the millennia of human life. *Why?* This simple, three-letter word represents a question that, under the limitations of human existence, is simply beyond our ability to answer, unless we are willing to do theological somersaults that leave God practically impotent.

But we are not left in this predicament alone. Wesley helps us with some forms of suffering. He rejects outright the thinking that if we sin, we will suffer, or if we are suffering, we must have sinned. We can find this line of thinking in some Christian circles even today, but our theology rejects such an idea. It is hard work to think through all the implications of suffering, but we must not blame the sufferers. Fortunately, Wesleyan theology, and the work of Wesley himself, gives us a healthy alternative. It comes out of his fine-tuned definition of perfection, and especially from his discussions of what Christian perfection is not.

What Christian Perfection Is Not

As adamant as John Wesley was about proclaiming Christian perfection, he was just as insistent on explaining what it is not. Most of the misunderstandings about Christian perfection can be clarified if we pay close attention to the distinctions he made. "A failure to distinguish between sin and infirmity puts an undue emphasis upon sin, and has a tendency to discourage earnest seekers from pressing on to a full deliverance from the carnal mind."[4] Indeed, one of the greatest discouragements that can come from the whole of Wesleyan-Holiness theology is to wrongly believe that God calls us to an absolute, angelic, or even Adamic perfection. We never become *more than* human. We become *more human* through sanctification. We never grow beyond temptation. Even Christ was tempted. We never rise above a lack of wisdom, errors, mistakes, or any number of infirmities we suffer in mind and body. God does not expect this from us. Leo Cox aids our understanding here: "Human imperfections must never be confused with an evil moral nature. . . . This area of imperfection between perfect love and perfect performance was not passed over lightly by Wesley."[5] We shall not pass over it here. For clarity, we will divide these distinctions from perfect love into three categories: involuntary transgressions, imperfections, and infirmities.

Involuntary Transgressions

Wesley often distinguished between what he called voluntary and involuntary transgressions.[6] Similarly, he talked about "sin properly so-called" and "sin improperly so-called."[7] What he wanted to suggest by these desig-

---

4. H. Orton Wiley, *Christian Theology, Vol. 2* (Kansas City, MO: Beacon Hill Press), 508.

5. Leo George Cox, *John Wesley's Concept of Perfection* (Kansas City, MO: Beacon Hill Press, 1964), 182.

6. Since Wesley developed the meaning of these distinctions over time, what is presented here should be seen as his most mature thought on the subject.

7. Wesley offers an explanation of these terms in a letter of May 31, 1771, to a recipient he calls Miss March: "There cannot be a more proper phrase than that you used, and I will understand your meaning; yet it is sure you are a transgressor still—namely, of the perfect, Adamic law. But though it be true all sin is a transgression of this law, yet it is by no means true on the other hand (though we have so often taken it for granted) that all transgressions of this law are sin: no, not at all—only all voluntary transgressions of it; none else are sins against the gospel law." Wesley, "To Miss March," *Letters of John Wesley*, May 31, 1771, http://wesley.nnu.edu/john-wesley/the-letters-of-john-wesley/wesleys-letters-1771/.

nations is that Christian perfection deals with the moral actions and the moral center of a person. Involuntary transgressions—or sin improperly so-called—are not moral failures. Wesley's definition of sin as a willful act against a known law is very much in play here. Such willful sins are those sins for which we are culpable.[8]

Involuntary transgressions do not change our relationship with God, while unrepented, willful sins need to be addressed in this regard. We may transgress or go against the ideal in situations, but often we miss the mark of the ideal because of our human limitations, not because of our purposefully rebellious choices. Randy Maddox explains: "To understand the difference one needs to recall Wesley's identification of will and affections. Potential imperfections of obedience flowing from wrong affections would be 'voluntary' because they are effected by the will and subject to our liberty; hence, they would be sinful. By contrast, infirmities are non-moral because they are involuntary; i.e., they are not subject to our concurrence (liberty)," or free-will.[9] Wesley himself writes:

> Another distinction to be kept in mind is that between humanity as such, and carnality. The latter is a perversion of the former. Entire sanctification does not remove any natural, normal, human trait, but it does purify these and bring them under subjection to the law of reason and the higher influences of divine grace. . . . I believe there is no such perfection in this life as excludes involuntary transgressions, which I apprehend to be naturally consequent on the ignorance and mistakes inseparable from mortality. There-

---

8. Technically speaking, Wesley does say that involuntary transgressions need the atoning blood of Christ in a general sense. But these actions do not change our relational status before God, whereas a willful act would.

9. Randy L. Maddox, *Responsible Grace: John Wesley's Practical Theology* (Nashville: Abingdon, 1994), 184.

fore, sinless perfection is a phrase I never use, lest I should seem to contradict myself. I believe a person filled with the love of God is still liable to involuntary transgressions.[10]

We must, however, think through the issue of responsibility for involuntary transgressions, particularly in our relationships with others. If we unintentionally hurt another person, we could use Wesley's ideas to the extreme and say we are innocent of the offense because we did not intend it. Clearly a relationship would never work in real life if based on some of the finer points we want to make theologically. Are we personally responsible for unintentional acts? We could say no in an effort to be theologically precise, but in real life, we take responsibility and apologize (or repent) when we have done harm, regardless of our intentions. Relationships suffer if we always declare ourselves innocent based on intentionality. Being in a relationship implies a generosity of spirit that takes responsibility for hurting others. This reality also applies to our relationship with God. Even unintentional acts should be confessed.

Imperfections

Imperfections can be distinguished from involuntary transgressions because the word "imperfection" is more general in meaning than what is implied in the word "transgression." Imperfections can lead to involuntary transgressions. Wesley observes,

> In what sense [are persons] not [perfect?] They are not perfect in knowledge. They are not free from ignorance, no, nor from mistake. We are no more to expect any living man to be infallible, than to be omniscient. They are not free from infirmities, such as weakness or slowness of understanding, irregular quickness or

―

10. Wesley, *A Plain Account of Christian Perfection* (Kansas City, MO: Beacon Hill Press of Kansas City, 1966), 54.

heaviness of imagination. Such in another kind are impropriety of language, ungracefulness of pronunciation; to which one might add a thousand nameless defects, either in conversation or behaviour. From such [imperfections] as these none are perfectly freed till their spirits return to God; neither can we expect till then to be wholly freed from temptation; for 'the servant is not above his master.' But neither in this sense is there any absolute perfection on earth.[11]

Wesley needed to clarify that Christian perfection does not raise us above our human limitations. We are not perfect in knowledge; we may even have intellectual difficulties. Christian perfection does not make us great orators or speakers. In countless ways we will always fall short of absolute perfection.

This distinction became crucial in what is known as the Perfectionist Controversy of the early 1760s. The leaders of the very influential Methodist Society in London began to preach a perfection that *was* absolute, or what they called "angelic," going against several of Wesley's own themes. First, this fanatical group believed that entire sanctification replaced any need for growth *prior* to it. Wesley always advised that entire sanctification is best pursued through attending to the means of grace. The person best prepared to receive the gift of entire sanctification is the one who has grown *toward* it through the various ways we nurture our relationship with God—daily prayer, Bible reading, and so on. Society leaders Thomas Maxfield and George Bell also rejected any need for growth *after* entire sanctification. The correct interpretation of Wesley's theology is that both gradual growth in grace and instantaneous entire sanctifi-

---

11. Wesley, *A Plain Account of Christian Perfection*, 23.

cation must be equally emphasized. One without the other on either side perverts the doctrine of Christian perfection.

Second, they suggested that only those who have been entirely sanctified are fit for heaven, thus wholly minimizing the power of new birth. Wesley quickly removed the leaders from the Society and began to preach more often against "angelic perfection."

Infirmities

Wesley also emphasized a different type of grace for human imperfections *not* addressed by saving or sanctifying grace—imperfections he called "infirmities." Whereas imperfections and involuntary transgressions are a normal part of human experience, the word "infirmities" implies something that has gone wrong in a more pervasive way than imperfections. Often, infirmities involve the body or the emotions—bodily ailments, disabilities, or mental illness. Wesley was ahead of his time in recognizing that these do not have their source in the sinful actions of the person whom they afflict. He was clear that infirmities do not affect one's salvation or relationship with God:

> We believe that there is no such perfection in this life as implies an entire deliverance, either from ignorance, or mistake, in things not essential to salvation, or from manifold temptations, or from numberless infirmities, wherewith the corruptible body more or less presses down the soul. We cannot find any ground in Scripture to suppose that any inhabitant of a house of clay is wholly exempt from bodily infirmities.[12]

We would do well to use this category of infirmities today in order not to blame victims, the disabled, the chronically ill, or the physically or emotionally sick for their suffering.

---

12. Wesley, *A Plain Account of Christian Perfection*, 36.

Christian perfection is a spiritual and moral condition. One can involuntarily transgress, display all sorts of imperfections common to being mortal, and suffer bodily or emotionally and still display perfect love. Wesley's point better fits today's biological, genetic, and psychological knowledge than a theological system that blames all suffering on the personal sin of the individual. It is not appropriate to tell a Christian hospitalized for a nervous breakdown that everything will be fine if they just confess their hidden sins. It is not appropriate to believe that persons suffer physically because they do not have enough faith. Living in a fallen world means we do not experience perfect human lives. But we can have perfect hearts that express themselves in love for God and others. Our infirmities may even keep us from expressing that love as fully as we would desire. But God looks at the intentions of the heart and sees the purity and perfection that have been effected through the *gift* of grace.

Holiness and Suffering

Many of us are familiar with Paul's physical struggle, which scholars believe might have been a painful eye condition. In 2 Corinthians 12 Paul called it a thorn in his flesh. He described his experience of asking God to heal him three times without relief. He attempted to make some sense of this difficult condition, searching for answers, as many of us do when we do not understand the suffering we must endure. Paul gives us a momentary glimpse into the whole realm of theodicy—a theological word that asks why a loving and powerful God would allow suffering—even the suffering of the innocent—in the world.

Paul himself testified to suffering on many fronts. Earlier in 2 Corinthians, Paul listed all the ways he suffered for Christ. That suffering seemed to have meaning for him, since he proclaimed that he suffered for the gospel (see 2

Corinthians 11). But chapter 12 feels different. Why a physical difficulty that could not be connected to his life as an apostle? This is different. In the end, he did not arrive at some ultimate answer that applies to us all, yet he did make his way *through* his own suffering and took the absurd meaninglessness out of his physical anguish. He plumbs the very depths of human experience and gives hope to all who feel forsaken in the pool of pain. But Paul does not answer the question "why." Rather, he answers the question "how." How do we endure? Simply put, Paul suggested a piece of wisdom that can touch even us: he said, paradoxically, that "[God's] power is made perfect in weakness" (v. 9), another one of the many Christian mysteries we call paradox. Here is the text in which we find these profound words:

> I was given a thorn in my flesh, a messenger of Satan, to torment me. Three times I pleaded with the Lord to take it away from me. But he said to me, "My grace is sufficient for you, for my power is made perfect in weakness." Therefore I will boast all the more gladly about my weaknesses, so that Christ's power may rest on me. That is why, for Christ's sake, I delight in weaknesses, in insults, in hardships, in persecutions, in difficulties. For when I am weak, then I am strong. (2 Corinthians 12:7b–10)

Our greatest temptation is to romanticize these words—to make them heroic by sanctifying—indeed, sterilizing—them. The phrases "God's grace is sufficient," "power is made perfect in weakness," and "when I am weak, then I am strong," should never be thrust upon someone who is suffering and should never imply what some inadequate theodicies do—that God gives us suffering for our own good. Rather, a deeper theological contextualization of Paul's words is crucial if we are to avoid the meaningless dead end of redeeming God by attempting to redeem, as onlookers, the suffering and pain of others. There is much we should not say about suffering. But, if we are to follow Paul, we can say grace—not sanctimoniously, but sacramentally. We can "say grace" by affirming the sufficiency of the grace and presence of God through the Holy Spirit.

What makes us Christian in the midst of suffering is the affirmation that God's grace is sufficient for us. In the midst of pain and suffering we may doubt the sufficiency of God's grace, but it is real. We have saving and sanctifying grace down, and we understand that we are saved by faith alone. And, even though we have had some theological problems at times with fully understanding that we are made holy by grace, for the most part we understand that we cannot sanctify ourselves—that it is God's work in us, a free gift as we open ourselves through continual consecration and surrender.

Yet we have not articulated well the sustaining grace of God. Perhaps we are uncomfortable with enduring suffering. We claim God's healing in every situation, and when it does not come to pass, we shove those who are suffering under the figurative rug. We cannot handle the fact that the suffering in our midst and across the world reminds us of our own mortality. We flee in fear—particularly in U.S. culture (and unlike most of the rest of the world)—at the thought of death. As a result, we sometimes abandon the sick and the chronically ill and the aged and the dying. We forget that, even though the Holiness denominations affirm divine healing, they have never encouraged a "name it and claim it" theology. We are to stand humbly before our God and accept that real human suffering continues regardless of how much faith we may muster.

Only as we bring such suffering into the light, out from under the rug, can we fully understand the significance of Christ's assurance that "my grace is sufficient for you." Theologically, we must affirm that the heart of God is present to the broken and the weak. God is with those who go without, who suffer physically, who suffer at the hands of others, who suffer from mental disease—and the list goes on and on. Jesus chose to spend his time with those who needed him most, and he repeatedly spoke of God's concern for the poor, the needy, the captive, the blind, the oppressed. To paraphrase him, *I did not come for the well, but for the sick* (see Matthew 9:12; Mark 2:17; Luke 5:31).

The heart of God is present to the weak in mysterious ways we do not often understand. Yet God is not only present—God is also powerfully active. It is here that we must redefine power. For those with infirmities who, for whatever reason, cannot "pick up their mats and walk" (see John 5:8, 11), an affirmation of God's power in the traditional sense seems like a cruel joke that they don't get. But if power is best characterized as God's self-emptying love for us, and if empowerment calls us to a self-emptying love for others, there breaks forth light in the midst of suffering.

My controversy with the church is that we often fail to do the hard work around the issues of suffering and holiness. Entire sanctification is not a cure-all! May we do better theologically so that we can do better practically— by loving those who suffer without questioning their holy devotion to God.

ELEVEN

Where Do We Go from Here?

For day after day they seek me out;
they seem eager to know my ways,
as if they were a nation that does what is right
and has not forsaken the commands of its God.
They ask me for just decisions
and seem eager for God to come near them.
"Why have we fasted," they say,
"and you have not seen it?
Why have we humbled ourselves,
and you have not noticed?"

Yet on the day of your fasting, you do as you please
and exploit all your workers.
Your fasting ends in quarreling and strife,
and in striking each other with wicked fists.
You cannot fast as you do today
and expect your voice to be heard on high.
Is this the kind of fast I have chosen,
only a day for people to humble themselves?
Is it only for bowing one's head like a reed
and for lying in sackcloth and ashes?
Is that what you call a fast,
a day acceptable to the Lord*?*

Is not this the kind of fasting I have chosen:
to loose the chains of injustice
and untie the cords of the yoke,
to set the oppressed free
and break every yoke?
Is it not to share your food with the hungry
and to provide the poor wanderer with shelter—
when you see the naked, to clothe them,
and not to turn away from your own flesh and blood?

—*Isaiah 58:2–7*

It has been identified in recent years that the Wesleyan-Holiness Movement is in the midst of an identity crisis. Even as far back as 1995, someone declared it "dead."[1] In one sense, it is not a new struggle. In the 1970s and '80s, some theologians thought the only way to survive long term was to "get back to Wesley." Others strongly maintained that the nineteenth-century Holiness Movement greatly *improved* on Wesley and that those distinctions should be tightly held. Though the voices have changed, some of the same sentiments still exist today, heightened by the cultural changes happening in the world around us. Social issues are hotly debated both outside and inside the church, and for Wesleyans, there is an even deeper identity issue: what makes us Wesleyan-Holiness?

Is it a set of theological positions we must all affirm?

Is it a historical entity to which we must be loyal?

Is it a set of practices, or, more precisely, a set of beliefs about certain practices in response to worldly culture that defines us?

Is it all of the above?

One thing is certain—disagreements about these realities rule the day. Is conformity necessary in all things, despite our geographical and cultural differences? If so,

---

1. See https://www.drurywriting.com/keith/dead.footnoted.htm.

how is that conformity administrated? If not, how do we handle our differences?

Where Is the Holiness Church Now?

The number of those who explicitly identify as Christian continues to fluctuate, including in those who have belonged to Wesleyan-Holiness denominations. In certain world areas the number is growing, especially in Africa and South America. In other places, there appears to be a sharp decline. Europe has been using the label "post-Christian" for some time now. Is it time to use this word in other parts of the world? While it is probably impossible to make generalizations about "the state of the church" globally, in light of the growth differences in different parts of the world, it is possible to identify that one of the factors affecting decline in the more post-Christian areas is that younger generations are increasingly disillusioned with the church.

We often see disagreement along generational lines over what is important in faith matters. Some in older generations think orthodoxy must be preserved at all costs. As anxiety and insecurity about the changing world increase, the tendency is to calcify doctrine. Conversely, many in younger generations find orthopraxis (how faith is lived out) to be the ultimate expression of their faith. What one *does* do as a result of their faith is more important to these believers than what one does *not* do. Theology and doctrine may become fluid to believers like this, who resonate strongly with the idea that a valid theology must work in real life and address actual situations. When a theology does not address real-life situations, these believers more readily question that theology's legitimacy, or even discard it altogether.

Yet it is not only younger generations who are questioning the wisdom of continued fidelity to the holiness message; many who lived through and were harmed by the Holiness Movement's more legalistic period are also questioning the usefulness of holiness theology as a whole, leading to unprecedented disillusionment about the church across multiple generational lines. They were presented with a god (lowercase) who is not the real God—the God of the universe, the God of Scripture, the God of Jesus. They were presented with a false God, absent of love, who really looks nothing like who God really is. Their view of God was formed—or, rather, malformed—by strong images of a god who was far from a God of love. Some were dealt a hand with a god quite unlike the God of Jesus—like a joker in a deck of cards. Many have been dealt a god who looks a lot like a god of legalism, a god who brings punishment and death, hopelessness and shame; a god who brings *disgrace*, instead of *grace*. With those ideas and in that ethos, a person's spirituality can be damaged. They may believe they are worthless—not in their mind, but deep down in their gut, where trauma lives. The question of what God is like is the most important question in all times, in all places; it is crucial that we reveal and embody the true God of Scripture, not a misdirected and damaging caricature of an angry and wrathful god.

The God of true holiness theology gives us a different message to share: God in Christ, through the Holy Spirit, is a God of infinite love, who shows us the lengths to which that love will go on the cross; a God of startling humility, who allowed himself to die for love of us and for the world. Jesus fully and finally reveals to us the nature of God.

God is the God who has done everything a God can do to heal us in our innermost parts, who has taken not only our sin but also our shame into himself in Christ.

God is the God who bends down and binds up our wounds.

God is the God of kindness, mercy, and unlimited grace.

God is the God who loves us as we are, who brings us to life and wholeness and holiness.

This is the divine Christ who shows us—reveals to us, by who he is and what he does—what the real God is really like.

Is this God at the heart of our message? If so, this God calls us further. The God of holiness theology and practice presses us to love our neighbors with this same divine love. Holiness is not holy living if it is not *wholly loving*. This is a compelling message; it is an empowering message; and it is the message that can counter the world's siren song that is devoid of any notion that we were created for love. The gospel message of the real God, that we in turn embody, will keep us from being "ineffective and unproductive," as Peter says. Indeed:

> His divine power has given us everything we need for a godly [holy] life through our knowledge of him who called us by his own glory and goodness. Through these he has given us his very great and precious promises, so that through them you may participate in the divine nature, having escaped the corruption in the world caused by evil desires. For this very reason, make every effort to add to your faith goodness; and to goodness, knowledge; and to knowledge, self-control; and to self-control, perseverance; and to perseverance, godliness; and to godliness, mutual affection; and to mutual affection, love. For if you possess these qualities in increasing measure, they will keep you from being ineffective and unproductive in your knowledge of our Lord Jesus Christ.
>
> (2 Peter 1:3–8)

The Diverse Church

If we take Paul seriously in his discussion of equality in the church in 1 Corinthians 12, we are to celebrate all kinds of diversity. Every part of the church is needed and interdependent on all the other parts. In other places, Paul writes very directly on the need for racial reconciliation between Jews and gentiles. In Galatians 3 he writes, "So in Christ Jesus you are all children of God through faith, for all of you who were baptized into Christ have clothed yourselves with Christ. There is neither Jew nor Gentile, neither slave nor free, nor is there male and female, for you are all one in Christ Jesus" (vv. 26–28). Devaluing or dehumanizing others is clearly not Christian. Referencing the Corinthian correspondence, Daniel Migliore writes:

> If Scripture is viewed primarily as a witness to God's liberating love in Christ . . . then the passing on of its liberating and transforming message must be a creative and critical process rather than a mechanical repetition. . . . The Bible is faithfully interpreted when it is read as a source of freedom in Christ to overcome every bondage, including the use of the Bible itself as a weapon of oppression."[2]

Donald Dayton was an important scholar of the Holiness Movement who died in 2020. In the prologue to his significant book, *Discovering an Evangelical Heritage*, he reflects on his own journey in the 1960s and beyond. After graduating from a Holiness college, he realized the extreme discrepancy and conflict between the norms of his college and the eruption of social issues during that tumultuous decade:

> The trauma generated by these conflicts was intense. Torn between evangelicalism and the imperatives of the Civil Rights Movement, I chose the latter. . . . I worked with the Mississippi Freedom Democratic party in the election of 1964. I lived with blacks [sic]

---

2. Daniel Migliore, *Faith Seeking Understanding* (Grand Rapids: Eerdmans, 2014), 57.

on the edge of Harlem during the riots of the summer of 1964 and identified in successive years with various black churches and inner-city ministries. . . . In several years of study and experience I found a reformulation in the recovery of a biblically grounded and classically Christian faith amenable to the development of social responsibility. . . . I took up the study of the roots of the denomination in which I had been reared. . . . I discovered much to my surprise that the denomination was a product of the closest parallel to the Civil Rights Movement in American history—the abolitionist protest against slavery in the pre-Civil War period. The founders of my denomination and college were advocates of principles in which I had come to believe by a very indirect route.[3]

The Holiness Movement's belief and practice of holiness led advocates to work for a pressing radical social agenda that included abolition of slavery, prohibition of alcohol (in the interest of curbing domestic abuse), women's right to vote, ministry to the poor in city missions, the establishment of orphanages and hospitals, and the inclusion of all races and both genders to ordination and every level of leadership in the general church.

Wesley's Methodists fed the poor and offered medical aid; worked for the education of children and argued against child labor; regularly visited prisoners and the sick; allowed women to preach; and showed deep compassion for the masses in general. Wesley also strongly argued against slavery in his preaching and writing. These actions of the Methodists in the 1700s carried on in Holiness circles in the 1800s. The question before us today is: what are Holiness people to do now about issues of race and the full

---

3. Donald W. Dayton, *Discovering an Evangelical Heritage* (New York: Harper & Row, 1976), 4.

equality of all persons in church and society on a practical level? Does our Holiness theology have anything to say? Is it still relevant?

After the killing of George Floyd in 2020, millions of people worldwide protested the death. Although awareness was already rising of too many innocent deaths of Black Americans at the hands of police, the videos captured and shared of Floyd struggling to breathe catapulted the issue to the forefront of a global conversation. Howard Thurman, in *Jesus and the Disinherited*, expresses the inconsistency between professed commitments of Christians and the stark historical reality of racial prejudice in their midst:

> This is the question which individuals and groups who live in our land always under the threat of profound social and psychological displacement face: Why is it that Christianity seems impotent to deal radically, and therefore effectively, with the issues of discrimination and injustice on the basis of race? Is this impotence due to a betrayal of the genius of the religion, or is it due to a basic weakness in the religion itself?[4]

A 2024 book by Wesleyan-Holiness scholars called *Awakening to Justice: Faithful Voices from the Abolitionist Past* answers Thurman's burning question: "The authors—as scholars who profess faith in Jesus Christ—believe that the lack of an adequate response to injustice is not a basic weakness in Christianity but indeed is a betrayal of the heart of the gospel message."[5] Scholars have not only identified the issues that concerned Holiness people in the nineteenth century but have also dug deeper to see that

---

4. Howard Thurman, *Jesus and the Disinherited* (Boston: Beacon Press, 1996), xix.

5. David D. Daniels III, Diane Leclerc, Christopher P. Momany, and Doug Strong, eds., *Awakening to Justice: Faithful Voices from the Abolitionist Past* (Downers Grove, IL: InterVarsity Press, 2024), 20. See also awakeningtojustice.com for the documentary made in conjunction with the book.

there are social implications in holiness theology itself that should guide us still.

Doug Strong, one of the editors and authors of *Awakening to Justice*, identifies some of the relevant beliefs held by Holiness abolitionists of the past:

> the belief that God initiates a relationship with individuals through a transforming experience with Jesus Christ (experiential conversion); the sentiment that Christians should practice a piety shaped by Scripture (biblically based devotion); the insistence that every person needs to turn away from their sin (repentant redemption); and the commitment that Christians need to express their faith publicly by sharing the gospel message with others and by conducting their everyday lives ethically (holy activism).[6]

This holy activism had very specific outcomes. The Holiness Movement was, on principle, abolitionist. Holiness denominations came into being with this tenet as their purpose. There was no hesitation to call slavery and racism a sin. This position should still be the unequivocal case for Holiness denominations today—not only out of a social vision but also out of the theology that informs that vision. Not only was the day of Pentecost used by early Holiness people as a metaphor for entire sanctification, but it was also seen and often articulated as a symbol of the full equality of all persons—young and old, slave and free, male and female will all prophesy equally.

The same sentiments that led Holiness people to an abolitionist position led almost all the denominations that formed out of the Holiness Movement to ordain women from the beginning, and to act on behalf of women more generally. Laws that kept women in positions with no rights were challenged by Holiness people; they worked for the

6. Daniels, et al., *Awakening to Justice*, 95.

Holiness is not holy living if
it is not *wholly loving*.

right of women to vote as a means of changing unjust and abusive laws, and they found it incongruent to work for the betterment of women in society while oppressing them in the church. Women's ordination was never challenged in Holiness churches—nearly a hundred years before even mainline liberal churches began to ordain women. It came also out of our interpretation of the day of Pentecost and our deep belief in the equality of all.

Another aspect of this equality shaped how Holiness people interacted with those in economic distress. One of the Holiness denominations, the Church of the Nazarene, identifies not only in its history but also in its present-day admonishments that it is a church with a particular calling to the poor. It relates this calling directly to the ministry of Jesus and his special relationship with the poor around him, as well as his commands to his disciples to carry on that type of relationship. That denomination even goes so far as to say it believes Christian holiness to be inseparable from meeting the needs of the economically disadvantaged and inseparable from actively working toward a more just and equitable society.

In addition to being committed to the dignity of all persons, those in Holiness traditions have also focused on what has been called an "optimism of grace." We are optimistic about what grace can do in the lives of individuals who are fully consecrated to God. We are just as optimistic about the potential for the transformation of society as a whole. This optimism has played itself out in a particular eschatology found in the Holiness Movement—the idea that Jesus will return when the church is truly the church by enacting kingdom principles in broader culture (especially held and practiced by the Salvation Army). Although many Holiness denominations have produced leaders and advocates for social change, the continued existence of sexism and racism in the hearts of many members of the

Holiness tradition shows us that there remains work for us to do.

The Divided Church

Racism and sexism are only two of the social issues that can divide us today. Pundits have identified the collapse of the moderate position in many societies. Where once moderates were most appealing to the majority of the population, moderation is now often perceived as "weakness." We now choose "sides" unequivocally, rather than seeking commonalities or compromise. This polarity in politics certainly reflects polarization of a deeper kind—dramatically different ideas about what we most value. We are polarized in our underpinning ideologies, our philosophies of life, our very worldviews. We might even argue that political and ideological devotion have reached the point of mimicking religious sentiment—a situation that alarmed us in the past in various forms (e.g., Nazi or Communist ideologies)—when one's ultimate concern, or faith, was placed in something other than God; one theologian calls this type of ungodly devotion "the demonic."[7]

Before we blame polarization and extremism on the secularization of culture, we must recognize that the church is not immune. The umbrella of Christianity has grown so large that we no longer think alike or act alike as a whole enough to retain any essential commonalities of the creedal past. Will the Wesleyan-Holiness tradition be able weather the storms of cultural polarization in its renewed search for its own identity? Maybe even more importantly in the grand scheme, can we reclaim the *via media* (middle way) of Wesleyanism and Holiness theology for the sake of Christianity itself?

---

7. See Paul Tillich, *Dynamics of Faith* (New York: Harper & Brothers Publishers, 1956).

The Holiness tradition is now perhaps uniquely positioned to identify and maintain a Christian center and act as peacemakers—but we must take up that mantle boldly, not letting non-essential disagreements thwart the purposes of unity and peace. Our questions should lead us to real answers that will take compassion and compromise seriously, rather than resulting in further entrenchment in our "sides."

Is there a true north? Is there a holiness ethic to guide us on so many issues? For example, how do we faithfully talk about creation care? How should we reconcile consumerism with the reality of poverty in our world? How should we address conversations on sexuality and gender expression while simultaneously confronting the problems of marital infidelity, pornography addiction, and sexual abuse within our own congregations, even among our clergy? How do we speak about abortion and the death penalty in holy ways?

We must acknowledge that there are different positions, even among Christians in the Holiness tradition, on some of these questions. Yet how can we be peacemakers if disagreements separate and divide people and churches within the Holiness Movement, and if our discourse has disintegrated below what could reasonably be considered charitable? Besides losing the credibility of our witness, the most dangerous effect is that such uncharitable arguing takes our focus away from God, away from the unity we have in Christ, and away from our specific calling in the world. John Wesley believed that God raised up and called the Methodist people to proclaim holiness around the world. May God empower us to do so today.

The Future Church

Yes, the world is complex, and ethical positions are difficult. But are we really left to our own devices and our own opinions about what a holiness ethic demands? It would do us well to return to Jesus's questions to the rich man as a primary ethical guide: are we willing to give away everything we have in order to keep God as God in our lives? In order to live out a holiness ethic, we prioritize the example of Jesus in his life and ministry as our primary standard. Only a church centered on Jesus and empowered by the Spirit can survive and thrive into the future.

On the night Jesus was betrayed, he took a towel and basin and washed his disciples' feet. We know that Jesus took the position of a slave in this act. Often this description is used to highlight the servanthood of Jesus. And, as Peter's question to Jesus suggests (John 13:6), this act of humility was supposedly not appropriate for a Messiah. Nevertheless, this very act of humility foreshadows the submission at Gethsemane, which leads to the trial and ends at the cross. Jesus could have lorded it over his disciples, demanding that *they* wash *his* feet; he could've resisted arrest in the garden; he could've pled his case at trial, fought back at his scourging, rejected the cross. But Jesus died. Jesus—the fully divine and fully human one—died a real, human death.

There is great significance in the fact that Jesus, with deep and pervasive humility, became "obedient to death— even death on a cross" (Philippians 2:8). Jesus underwent the totality of the human experience and saw it through to its end, which shows us his expansive and inexhaustible empathetic capacity toward us. The truest expression of the extent of his love was that Jesus emptied himself, laid down his life for his friends, and was entombed. Moreover, it must not be forgotten that he died *on a cross*—the most graphic and elucidatory symbol of guilt and shame in that culture at that time. He died the most humiliating death imaginable.

"Whoever wants to be my disciple must deny themselves and take up their cross daily and follow me. For who-

Holiness is not just a theology.
It lives and breathes and acts.

ever wants to save their life will lose it, but whoever loses their life for me will save it" (Luke 9:23–24). These verses are extremely familiar to us as holiness people who believe that consecration and surrender are the means to entire sanctification. Yet, while we have made ourselves experts at self-denial (all those "thou shalt nots"), we have not always understood the call to pick up our crosses. We have interpreted it to mean that we have a cross to carry from time to time—an illness to bear, or some period of personal struggle. We forget that Jesus's cross was a complete and final sacrifice on behalf of the other. We take up our crosses when we suffer on behalf of *others*! Further, we misunderstand Jesus if we lose our lives *in order to* save ourselves! Securing our own salvation should be the result—not the motivation. The call, then, is to pour out our hearts and our lives as Christ poured out his—on behalf of those who cannot save themselves.

The call to self-sacrifice and self-emptying is not a political agenda. It is the biblical mandate. Like Christ, we are called to feed the hungry, clothe the naked, heal the sick, give sight to the blind, free the oppressed, and proclaim the year of the Lord. The biblical mandate leads us to fight injustice, resist any disregard of human dignity, and perhaps work against public policy that stands against the marginalized. We understand these things more deeply and are better able to discern the ethic of Christian action when our orthodoxy is Christocentric, and our orthopraxis truly Christlike. Those who were part of the Wesleyan revival in Great Britain and the early Holiness Movement in the United States seemed to understand these things because their hearts were reflections of the heart of Jesus. Will we allow such understandings to guide us into the future?

We end as we began—with the Sermon on the Mount. Unlike most evangelicals, Wesleyan-Holiness theology proclaims that the Sermon on the Mount can be lived out by those fully devoted to God. It is a guide to a truly holy ethic—a truly Wesleyan-Holiness ethic. But holiness is not just a theology. It lives and breathes and acts. Just as Jesus called the rich man to give up everything he desired most, so too are we called to give up our idols—whether it be money or something else we hold dearly—in order to follow Jesus and his call to love, no matter the cost. This is the heart of holiness. It must be in the hearts of holiness people too.

May it be so with us, Lord. May it be so.